INTO the BREACH

Memoirs of a Newfoundland Senator

Frederick W. Rowe

McGRAW-HILL RYERSON LIMITED
Toronto   Montreal

Care has been taken to trace the ownership of any copyright material contained in this text; however, the publishers will welcome information that enables them to correct any reference or credit in subsequent editions.

The photographs in this book are from the author's private collection.

ISBN   0-07-549669-0

Canadian Cataloguing in Publication Data

Rowe, Frederick W., 1912–
    Into the breach: memoirs of a Newfoundland senator

Includes index.
ISBN 0-07-549669-0

1. Rowe, Frederick W., 1912– . 2. Canada. Parliament. Senate — Biography.   3. Legislators — Canada — Biography.   4. Politicians — Newfoundland — Biography.   5. Newfoundland — Politics and government — 1949– . I. Title.

FC626.R68A3 1988   328.71'092'4   C88-094575-3
F1034.3.R68A3 1988

1 2 3 4 5 6 7 8 9 10 W 7 6 5 4 3 2 1 0 9 8

Printed and bound in Canada by Webcom Limited.

CONTENTS

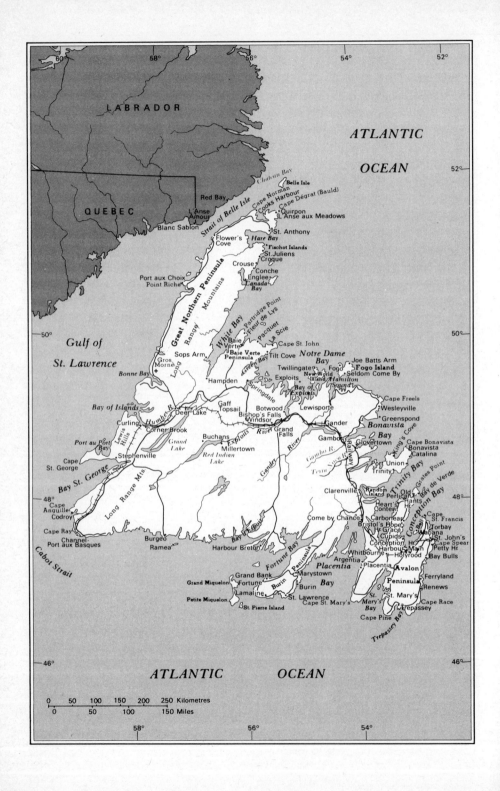

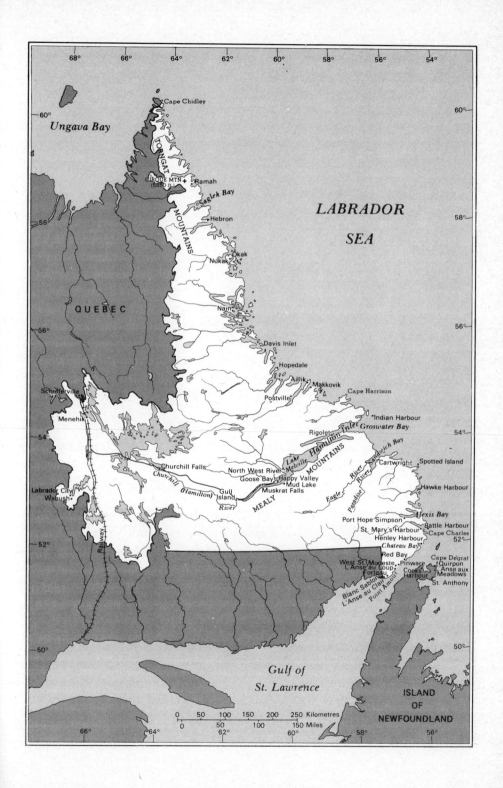

Preface

Inevitably, in a book purporting to be "memoirs" there will be portions which leave some readers dissatisfied, and indeed irritated, that they were induced to devote a significant amount of time to what they might consider trivial and inconsequential. It is well known that we are living in an age when increasing demands are made on our time — this is particularly true when it comes to reading. So I suggest that readers of the present work be on the lookout for such passages and that they do not hesitate to use a firm hand in exempting them from serious attention.

But having made this point, I would presume to draw the attention of potential readers to two important principles related to the above. One is that, even in the field of literature, minorities have rights which should not be ignored, and among these is the right to read whatever the individual wishes to read. Of course, one must have due regard to the security of the state, but this reservation should be applied only in the gravest circumstances; if there is one thing I have learned over the years, it is that those who invoke one such protective device are rarely willing to stop there.

The second point I wish to make here — though at the risk of being considered a little pompous — is that in evaluating personal writing of the kind found in this book, one has to be careful not to throw out the baby with the bath water. What seems insignificant in one period may be considered extremely valuable in another. History is replete with examples of music, sculpture, painting, and above all, literature that were deemed inconsequential only to be regarded totally differently later on. In fact, this has happened so often that we should observe the utmost caution in placing evaluations, whether negative or positive, on new contributions in these fields.

The writing of one's memoirs is not as easy or satisfying as it appears at first sight. The problem is not the inadequacy of material but rather the superfluity, not the difficulty of finding information but rather the embarrassment of having to omit or discard much of the formidable amount available. Readers of this book will note that I have given considerable space to my original home, Lewisporte. But what is not so obvious is that I could have devoted the entire book to this village, which did not attain a population of 700 until the start of World War II.

It is not only because it was my home for 23 years that Lewisporte occupies a dominating position in this book. The town has come to be important in its own right. When Lewisporte was founded in the 1870s, the majority of the settlers were still fishermen. Within a few years, a considerable number of them were part-time farmers; then lumbering became important, followed by logging for pulpwood. Most important of all was the establishment, around the end of the century, of Lewisporte as a rail and steamship centre, one that is second only to St. John's and Port aux Basques. And finally, in the late 1930s came the need to service Gander, one of the world's great airports, a need made permanently visible by the great oil tanks, the largest in the province, that dominated the Lewisporte landscape.

This book is not meant to be a history of the several towns that, in addition to Lewisporte, are discussed by me in some detail — Bonne Bay, Bishops Falls, Wesleyville, and St. John's — nor is it meant to be a dissertation on those political districts — Labrador, White Bay, and Grand Falls — which I had the pleasure of representing in the Newfoundland legislature.* However, various aspects of education and politics are dealt with in substantial detail, for the very obvious reason that I have spent nearly all my adult life in these fields. Here again I have laid myself open to the charge of being arbitrary and capricious in my selection. So be it.

Another criticism likely to emerge as the book is examined in some detail is that I have been somewhat overgenerous in my treatment of the Rowe family. In this case I run the risk of being accused of a mild form of nepotism. In my defense I would point out that the Rowe family is one of the oldest in England, with roots dating back to William the Conqueror. Branches of the family are no longer confined to the West Country but have spread over the British Isles and from there to every part of the English-speaking world. In a broad and general way I have tried to tell some portions of their story. And other Newfoundlanders, I am glad to say, have done likewise, though the story of some of these families — English, Welsh, Irish, and Scottish — is still waiting to be told. If this, probably the last of my books, encourages the trend, I shall feel more than gratified.

Frederick W. Rowe

---

* The reader will perhaps notice a few inconsistencies in the spelling of the names of towns between the map and the text of this book. This is of no consequence as the variant forms are all correct and in use by Newfoundlanders. The map was prepared for my *History of Newfoundland and Labrador.*

Acknowledgements

I have received help and encouragement from a number of people, to whom I extend my thanks: Senator M. Lorne Bonnell, Derek Bursey, Stanley Butt, Ethel E. Colbourne, Mona Cramm, Dr. Harry Cuff, Thomas Dale, Richard H. Ellis, Rosalind Godfrey, Stuart Godfrey, Nancy Granville, Dr. Gordon Handcock, Dr. Leslie Harris, Anne Hart, Senator Henry Hicks, Hon. Gerald Hill, Dr. James Hiller, Bishop R. J. Lahey, David Leamon, Senator Derek Lewis, Aiden Maloney, Rachel Mansfield, Eva Melanson, Dr. Thomas Nemic, Hon. T. Anthony Paddon, Hon. J. W. Pickersgill, Benjamin Powell, Norma Jean Richards, Bobbie Robertson, the Rowe family—especially Harold U. Rowe, Kenneth C. Rowe, Melvin Rowe, and William S. Rowe—Eric Spicer, Senator David Walker, Captain Earl Winsor, and Rev. Naboth Winsor.

This book has been published in part with the help of a grant from the Social Services and Humanities Research Council of Canada, to whom I would also like to express my gratitude.

To my wife, Edie

"Once more unto* the breach, dear friends, once more. . . ."

William Shakespeare
King Henry the Fifth, III, i, 1

---

* Often loosely quoted as "into."

Introduction

I was born in 1912 in the northern Newfoundland village of Lewisporte in Notre Dame Bay. When this settlement was founded, by a group of Methodist families of which my maternal grandfather's family was one, it was called Burnt Bay. The name was changed around the turn of the century.

The community of Lewisporte was church-dominated, which probably explains why educational standards were relatively high. Nowhere was John Wesley's emphasis on education more evident than in the work the pioneer settlers of Burnt Bay put into building a log cabin to accommodate a visiting clergyman and a teacher. The role played by churches of various denominations in establishing and maintaining a measure of civilization in those small, isolated communities of Newfoundland has not been fully recognized; I intend to remedy that to some extent.

Both my parents came from villages on Fogo Island: my father from Seldom-Come-By and my mother from Joe Batts Arm. My father's parents were Anglican, but since there was no Anglican*

---

* For convenience I will use the modern term "Anglican" to refer to the church that has been known until recent times as the Church of England.

church in Burnt Bay my father supported the Methodist (later the United) Church all his life.

My personal history is rooted deep in Newfoundland history and culture and my earliest recollections go back to the final years of World War I (I was six when that war ended), the political and economic upheavals of the 1920s, and the Depression of the 1930s. When I was older I followed the financial collapse of Newfoundland, and the installation of the Commission of Government (a political experiment of increasing interest to scholars, especially political scientists).

My career has been a variegated one. I have been a school teacher; a supervising inspector of schools; a university lecturer; a Confederation protagonist; a co-founder of Newfoundland's Department of Public Welfare; Deputy Premier of Newfoundland; a graduate of four institutions of higher learning; a chairman or member of numerous governmental bodies; the author of articles and books dealing with Newfoundland's history and culture; a 20-year member of the Newfoundland legislature (and holder of a record number of political portfolios); a 16-year member of the Senate of Canada; and a senatorial delegate to Italy, Sri Lanka, Pakistan, the Council of Europe (Strasbourg), the Bahamas, Korea, China, UNESCO (Paris), and the United States.

As a youth, to complete my matriculation requirements, I went to St. John's to attend Prince of Wales College in 1929. I graduated from the Normal School, a teacher training institution, in 1930, which marked the beginning of a career of teaching and other educational activities, interrupted occasionally by breaks for continuing my education. Between 1929 and 1949, I was a teacher or principal at Bonne Bay, Bishops Falls, Lewisporte, Wesleyville, Grand Bank, and St. John's. Also, at various times I attended Memorial University College, Mount Allison University, and the University of Toronto, and for eight years I lectured to teachers during the summer sessions of Memorial.

My public service and political career started in 1947 when I publicly supported Joseph Smallwood in his fight for Confederation by participating in debates (then a popular diversion), writing letters to the press, and giving talks over the radio. In 1949 I became the first Deputy Minister of Public Welfare in the Newfoundland government, and for the following three years, under the Minister, the Honourable Dr. H. L. Pottle, I supervised the implementation of all the new provincial welfare measures and cooperated with federal authorities as they in turn undertook, almost overnight, similar actions at the federal level.

In 1952 I joined the Smallwood Cabinet, serving, as I have said, in a record number of portfolios: Mines and Resources, Public Welfare, Education, Highways, Finance, Community and Social Development, Labrador Affairs, President of the Council, and Deputy Premier. My successive electoral districts were all of Labrador; White Bay South; and Grand Falls—in that order. In the course of some 20 years, my ministerial duties included major programs: administration of mining exploration; the creation of royal commissions on forestry and on agriculture; creation of the Royal Commission on Wildlife; the elimination of bovine tuberculosis and brucellosis from Newfoundland cattle; and the introduction of moose to Labrador. I was also responsible for a blueprint for education which included recommending a new university campus; a technical and vocational program; the most generous program in Canada of scholarships and bursaries for high school and university students; and the consolidation of schools and boards of education.

As Minister of Highways, I supervised the building of over one-half of the province's share of the Trans-Canada Highway, and introduced many programs of secondary roads and bridges and a paving and road program which by the 1970s had virtually eliminated Newfoundland's historic isolation.

As Minister of Finance, I modernized and rationalized the liquor laws of the province; served as chairman of the governing committee of the Come Home Year project, which I had recommended to Cabinet and which, almost overnight, doubled and later trebled the tourist industry of the province. In the 1960s I served, at Smallwood's request, as chairman of all the educational and regional conferences, and supervised the initial resettlement and centralization programs. During this period I also chaired the conference that recommended free university tuition, allowances for university students, provincial allowances to mothers with children in school, and a special program for retarded and handicapped children.

Through the years a number of honours and degrees have been conferred upon me. In 1936 I was elected valedictorian at Memorial. This gave me great pleasure, because during those years, and even until at least 1949, it was extremely difficult for an outport Newfoundlander to obtain that honour.

I was recipient of the O. E. Smith Scholarship at Mount Allison

University. In 1949 I received a graduate degree of Bachelor of Pedagogy with honours from the University of Toronto. It had been an arduous course and I felt pleased beyond measure. From there I went on to try for, and obtain, what was generally regarded as one of Canada's more difficult degrees: Doctor of Pedagogy.

My doctorate led indirectly to another, less academic form of recognition. When I proposed my doctoral thesis on the history of education in Newfoundland, I was overjoyed that the university authorities accepted it, and authorized the publication of the usual abstracts. When the thesis was completed, one of my professors in graduate studies urged me to make further use of the material I had accumulated. Reminding me of the gross lack of Newfoundland information in Canada — a lack that became more obvious as union of Newfoundland and Canada became a reality — he suggested I contact one or two Toronto publishers.

As a Methodist and, later, a United Church man, I was familiar with the religious publications of the Ryerson Press, named after Methodist writer and theologian Egerton Ryerson. As it happened, the Ryerson Press was then established quite near the University of Toronto, and the head of the firm was Dr. Lorne Pierce, one of Canada's outstanding scholars of that time. Dr. Pierce was most courteous to me during our meeting, and when I was leaving he asked me if he might take the manuscript home for a day or two. Of course I agreed, but I was a little disconcerted to have a call from him the next morning asking if I could come to see him. I feared the worst, but went anyway. When I arrived at his office, he said the Ryerson Press was interested in publishing my manuscript. That was the beginning of my long association with what eventually became McGraw-Hill Ryerson, one of the great publishing houses of the world. I regarded the decision of Ryerson to publish my *History of Education in Newfoundland* at a time when I was completely unknown to them as an honour of the highest rank.

Among other honours that give me great satisfaction are the Heritage Award from the Newfoundland Historical Society, the Certificate of Merit from the Canadian Historical Association, and honourary membership in the Newfoundland Teachers' Confederation.

In the spring of 1982 Dr. Leslie Harris, the president of Memorial University, contacted me to say that my name had been submitted by the university senate for an honourary degree, the

Litt.D. *honoris causa*. This was a surprise, and of course very gratifying. We have only one university but it is one of which the vast majority of Newfoundlanders are intensely proud. The thing that made me still more proud was Dr. Harris's inviting me to give the convocation address, the equivalent of the 1936 honour.

It was not vanity that made me so proud that pleasant afternoon six years ago. Rather, it was the fact that there on the campus was the visible evidence of Newfoundland's fantastic growth of recent years. Starting almost from nothing, we had built that great university which today can sit alongside all the great universities of Canada. I cannot help feeling, too, that the degree that gave me the greatest sense of achievement was the humble B.A.* There, I and other Newfoundlanders broke the academic sound barrier. No longer did we look enviously at the academic achievements of others. Those achievements now belonged to us and not just to the favoured few.

I have been unable to find out when the Rowes settled first in Newfoundland, for two reasons. First, like many others from the West Country of England, my ancestors first became familiar with Newfoundland by coming out in fishing schooners in the spring and returning in the fall. The second reason is the fact that long before the first Rowes settled in Newfoundland they were to be found all along the south coast of England from Cornwall to Kent. By the middle 1600s they had penetrated to northern England, Scotland, and Ireland, but it is significant that those who had taken up residence in London (such as Owen Rowe, the regicide, and Nicholas Rowe, the poet laureate) had definite connections with the West Country.

Another factor making it difficult to trace my genealogy was that, apparently, very early in the Rowes' association with Newfoundland four distinct groups could be identified. There were the Rowes of Trinity and Hearts Content, those of Carbonear, those of Cupids and vicinity, and those of St. John's. By the early 1800s other groups could be identified. My own grandfather, for example, was born in Trinity in 1806 but by the 1830s had become a prominent planter of Seldom, from whom the Rowes of

---

* Of course, every student trying to obtain a university degree must have a subject to serve as the major; mine was in history and my "minor" was in English. The history-English combination has served me well, especially in my writing career.

Lewisporte (my family), as well as many of the St. John's Rowes, are derived.

I have done a fair amount of research into the Rowe background, but I make no apologies, for apart from personal considerations it seems to me that any family that has accumulated at least 17 coats of arms deserves recognition. In his *Lives of the Poets*, Dr. Johnson states that one coat was awarded by the King (most likely Richard the Lion-Hearted) to the ancestor of the poet Nicholas Rowe "for his services in the Holy Wars" (almost certainly the Crusades). The Rowe family also produced three Lords Mayor of London, a regicide who, according to *The Dictionary of National Biography*, took part between wars in the foundation of Massachusetts and the Bermudas, and the poet laureate whose statue stood in Poets' Corner in Westminster Abbey for over 250 years.*

It is not my intention to bore the reader with too many details about the Rowes, but the fact is that the Rowes were one of the first families to settle in Newfoundland, and from the earliest days they played a significant role in professional, business, and political life. Moreover, their descendants, hundreds of whom have spread to various parts of the province and thousands of whom have spread across Canada and the United States, would probably be interested in knowing more about their ancestry.

As I began my work on this book, I found — as one would expect with such an old family — that a considerable amount of research had already been done, some of it in the West Country and some in London. But more deserved to be done, especially to unearth the early relationship between the ship-fishery to Newfoundland and the permanent settlers. To this end I made a further visit to London and the West Country to examine once more the old records in such institutions as the Dorset County Records Office, the British Museum, and the Public Records Office in London.†

But I did not confine my research to the Rowe family. On my

---

* Because of overcrowding, Rowe's statue, along with that of several other well-known poets, was moved to another part of the Abbey about ten years ago.

† Previously, I had visited England on several occasions to obtain material for use in my several books. In this connection I visited the British Museum, the Dorset County Records Office, and, in particular, the Tower of London, where the well-known regicide, Owen Rowe, was imprisoned, and where he died (Charles II having, for some reason I was unable to find out, delayed signing or refused to sign his death warrant).

mother's side is another old West Country family name, the Freakes (traditionally pronounced FRAKES). They, too, had an interesting background which is part of my heritage as well as that of my children and grandchildren. But then in any study of a family genealogy the wife and mother should get equal billing. This is not too difficult in my wife's case, since her maiden name, Butt, is that of one of the most distinguished of the older settlers, about whom much material has already been accumulated. On her mother's side is the old and well-known Crocker family, who, like the Butts, were first domiciled in the Carbonear area. All three of these family names originated in the West Country of England.

In any case I would hope not to be restricted very tightly to personal and family allusions but would wish to follow the pattern that I have used for several of my other books: *Extinction*, *The Smallwood Era*, and *Education and Culture in Newfoundland*. In this way I hope to reach beyond personal history and bring together sociological and environmental factors which, when shorn of the mythology that has inevitably accumulated over the years, are revealed as having been instrumental in making the culture and life of Newfoundland unique in so many ways.

PART 1

FAMILY ORIGINS, CHILDHOOD, AND YOUTH 1912–1929

chapter
1   *Early Lewisporte*

The Burnt Bay that my father, Eli Rowe, and his mother and half-brothers moved into was as primitive a place as one could find in Newfoundland around 1882. A look at the map shows that Burnt Bay was relatively isolated from the great fishing communities of Twillingate, Exploits, and Fogo—places from which one looked for summer work either as an indentured servant in the inshore fishery or as a crewman on a Labrador schooner. Like many other places in Newfoundland, Burnt Bay got its name because of a fire in the area. (*The Gazetteer of the Island of Newfoundland* published by the Department of Mines and Technical Surveys in 1961 lists 68 place names that use "Burnt.")

Burnt Bay had certain assets that were denied to most of the islands of Notre Dame Bay—forests to the water's edge and, once the trees had been cut down for lumber or firewood, land with enough soil to justify cultivation, given the kelp and caplin (a small fish related to the smelt) for fertilization.

A century or two ago, Newfoundland's virgin forests were for the most part made up of spruce, balsam fir, white birch, and, above all, white pine—the pine of our "pine-clad hills." Until the early 1900s, my father and other residents of Burnt Bay could cut schooner spars where the main street of Lewisporte runs today, that is, about 200 feet from the salt water. How large were these trees? About 50 years ago, while I was in the woods (where the Masonic Temple now stands) I noticed a flat, round object covered with moss. I picked the moss away and uncovered solid wood, the stump of a pine tree that had been sawn by pit saw, and it was about three feet in diameter. Also, some years ago when our old family house was being demolished it was discovered that the boards of the back porch wall were 18 inches in width. But after the great forest fire of the early 1900s, no pines regenerated. The deciduous trees took precedence, followed by the spruce and fir. Lewisporte ceased being one of the leading schooner-building ports of northeastern Newfoundland.

One of the strong reasons for the movement of people from islands and outside harbours to Lewisporte was that in general there was more soil for agriculture. This soil was not, of course, readily available, since it was covered by an almost impenetrable forest. But the virgin forest that confronted the earliest settlers was soon decimated, and in time virtually destroyed, by a succession of fires; this fact also made it much easier for the would-be farmer to clear the land of stumps. A bigger problem was the existence of rocks and boulders; it was simply impossible to cultivate the land while the rocks remained on and in the soil. Since there were no tractors or other machines to facilitate this work, it had to be done either by human hands or by human hands assisted by animals.

Once the land was improved by clearing trees and rocks from it, however, one more great problem remained. Probably because of the preponderance of coniferous trees, the Newfoundland soil has always been extremely acidic. This was partially solved by keeping animals and poultry so that their dung could be used to make the soil more alkaline and by using caplin, squid, and other surplus fish for fertilizer, both of which processes tended to build up the soil over the years.

My maternal grandfather, James Freake, unlike his brother, had no boys old enough to assist in clearing the land. His three teenaged girls had no choice but to help if the ensuing year was to produce the basic crops of potatoes, turnips, and carrots. My mother has told me that one of the happiest days of her life was when her father returned from a trip to Exploits and informed the family that he had acquired a young ox, thus freeing the girls from the backbreaking drudgery of pulling stumps.

The nearest estimate for the year of the permanent founding of Burnt Bay is 1876, when Robert Woolfrey, with other members of his family, decided to stay there year-round instead of returning to Moretons Harbour on New World Island every spring as they had done for some time. The following year, the Freakes from Joe Batts Arm on Fogo Island also moved in permanently. There were two Freake families, those of Elijah and James. James Freake became my grandfather.

There were several reasons for these families to move, some of them economic. But in the case of the Freakes, another strong reason was a religious one. Although they had been among the first Methodists to establish themselves in Notre Dame Bay, they were a small minority surrounded by a sometimes hostile majority — especially when rum was readily available. On several occasions there was property violence of serious proportions ending in attempts to destroy James Freake's house. The Freakes would probably have moved off Fogo Island eventually, without any encouragement from anti-Methodist elements, but my mother, who at the age of seven had been an unwilling spectator to a bad incident, was always quite adamant that it was religious hostility which led to the final migration, a view shared by many of the non-Methodists.

Once it became clear that the Woolfreys and then the Freakes were moving in to stay, Burnt Bay started to grow, and by 1891, only 15 years or so after the Woolfreys had begun to stay all winter, the population of Burnt Bay was 235. After building their own tilts and houses, the settlers agreed on several necessities — a church, a church school, and a day school — but at first, one building had to serve all purposes.

Not all the settlers chose to live on the north side of the harbour; the Northcotts, Smalls, Martins, Leydens, Snows, and Jeans, for example, settled on the south side. But that community never reached the point where the normal community services could be demanded and expected, so the people on the south side resorted to horse or oxen and cart to carry produce of one kind or another. They did this even around the harbour, which meant travelling about three miles over a very rough road (the harbour was a mile wide and generally had to be crossed by rowboat). After World War I, and even before, newcomers to Lewisporte selected the north side as the better place to live; moreover, settlers who were already established on the south side generally decided to move to the north.

In addition to the Woolfreys and Freakes, the new settlers who selected the north side were N. Turner, Eli Rowe, Matthew King, and the Osbournes, Russells, Moyles, Rideouts, Pellys, Hanns, Laytes, Hodders, Boones, Manuels, and Bennets. Most of these names can be traced to Trinity Bay, and to some extent Conception Bay. Most of them had been in Notre Dame Bay for only a century or so before moving into the bottoms of the bays and forsaking the small island and mainland communities. Before establishing themselves on Newfoundland's "English Shore" (from Cape Race to Cape Bonavista) these names were to be found in the West Country of England. The great majority of the first settlers of the northeast coast had first settled in Conception, Trinity, and Bonavista Bays, and before that they had their homes in Devon, Dorset, and other West Country counties.

By the turn of the century the names "Burnt Bay" and "Marshallville" had disappeared as formal designations, in favour of "Lewisporte," after Lewis Miller, the Scottish entrepreneur who had made Lewisporte the chief shipping port for his pine-cutting operations in Glenwood and Millertown.

Between 1876 and 1901 (when the transinsular railway was built) the labourers of Burnt Bay fished during the summer and resorted to logging, trapping, and hunting during the fall and winter. Of these supplementary activities the most important was the logging and lumbering; in the latter part of the 18th century, sawmilling had become a leading activity. Fishing, of course, was often a failure thanks to bad weather, shipwreck, and, above all, ice. The knowledge that at Glenwood or Norris Arm or some other, smaller places there were sawmills looking for good loggers or good cooks (as my father was in his younger days) relieved some of the uncertainty often attached to the fisheries.

Burnt Bay was not a fishing community in the sense that places on the outside were. Because of this the tendency was for fishermen to go to one of the larger fishing settlements like Twillingate and "ship" for the Labrador fishery. This meant, of course, that they could be cut off from home and family for up to six months.

But worse than the actual separation was the psychological burden carried by those left at home. The Labrador fishery and its concomitant, the seal fishery, was one of the most hazardous on earth. The ships, schooners usually weighing 40 to 50 tons, depended on wind for propulsion. The crew would leave home in late May or early June and were very lucky if they met with no drift ice en route. Such ice could tie up a vessel for weeks and its pressure sometimes led to the destruction of the schooner. Once, my father got jammed in the Strait of Belle Isle, one of the roughest places in the world; the 30-ton vessel was rafted totally out of water for 21 days. That the ship was not a total loss with no survivors was simple luck. A heavy steel sealer happened to catch sight of them and came to their aid. She ploughed the ice around the schooner and then helped the small boat adjust to the water. (Boats subjected to such pressure were often damaged so seriously that when the ice broke up the boat would sink almost immediately.)

Equally dangerous to the fishermen were the wind and fog. Rarely did a summer pass without some loss of both ships and lives, and when the great hurricanes struck such losses could be staggering. Until this century, there was no communication whatever with the schooners that left Newfoundland in May and sailed north, until they returned in October. Sometimes neither ship nor crew ever returned; sometimes the crew were rescued but the schooner and its load of fish were lost.

Understandably, my mother hated the sea and everything connected with it. For a wife and family to have to wait three or four months to find out whether the husband and father had drowned was not only a form of economic slavery, but also psychological torture which no dependants should be called on to bear.

I was born on September 28, 1912, and the next day my father arrived home and informed my mother that he was finished with the sea. From then on he would be a land-based general manager for his brother-in-law's rapidly expanding business activities. I am sure that not even the birth of another boy brought the happiness to my mother that his announcement did. Periodically my mother would have bad dreams, and it is an indication of the traumatic hold that the sea had on her that the majority of her nightmares had to do with the the sea in one way or another.

My father had been a fisherman and fishing captain for 32 years. For seven or eight of those years he was a "coaster" or "trader." This meant that he was no longer a fisherman, but he encountered the same dangers. To exchange fish for other commodities called for almost constant marine travel, and on three occasions he was shipwrecked. One was during the great hurricane known euphemistically as the "September gale" — actually a storm which in Twillingate harbour alone wrecked 26 of the 27 schooners vainly seeking shelter there.

Two of the most tragic of Newfoundland's sealing disasters took place in 1912 when 78 men of the S.S. *Newfoundland* froze to death and the S.S. *Southern Cross* was lost with all 195 hands, for a total of 273 dead during the 24-hour period. In both cases the tragedy was aggravated by the agonizing hope that some lives might be saved. In the case of the *Southern Cross* no sign of the ship or her crew was ever seen.

Another aspect of the Labrador and seal fisheries has been alluded to earlier. The average Newfoundlander living in the outports occupied a house that had no plumbing or central heating. This was doubly hard on those wives whose husbands fished on the Labrador coast in the summer and engaged in logging in the winter. What with mending nets, repairing boats, etc. there was literally not enough time for the man to do what needed to be done. Of course, if there was a teenaged boy in the family he came into the picture, but often at the expense of his schooling.

What was it like to grow up in early Lewisporte? Perhaps my mother would serve as a good model of the people and their lives. Phoebe Ann Freake was the youngest daughter of James Freake of Joe Batts Arm. She was born in March at a time when her family were spending the winter at Scissors Cove, a small logging community near Burnt Bay. Her family did not move permanently to Burnt Bay until she was about seven years old.

The first teacher in the first school at Burnt Bay was Maria Woolfrey. Even though her own education was limited, she pursued her calling with a dedication that stimulated and encouraged learning. My mother started attending Maria Woolfrey's school as soon as her family settled in Burnt Bay. She was considered "pretty smart" by her classmates, and in short order she became an insatiable reader, being held back only by the paucity of reading material in this small and only partially literate village. (Fortunately, children of my mother's generation in Burnt Bay all became literate, in sad contrast to the great majority of children in other communities.) That my mother had been one of Maria Woolfrey's students no doubt accounted for the omnivorous reading that characterized her long life of 87 years. (An hour or so before her death in the General Hospital in St. John's, she was immersed in the current issue of the *National Geographic*.)

My mother lived at home until she married Eli Rowe at the age of 18. Very little work was available to her outside her home, because Burnt Bay was still a very small community at the end of the century.

Mother was a practising Methodist and therefore a steady reader of the Bible. Her favourite readings were in the Psalms, many of which she knew by heart, and when the opportunity presented itself she did not hesitate to read — actually recite — some of her favourites. Unfortunately, not for many years did we realize that my mother had recognized what was, regardless of anyone's religious belief, some of the noblest poetry handed down to us over the ages.

The majority of children of school age did go to school. In this, Lewisporte resembled a number of other small communities where school attendance, while not compulsory, was a moral obligation. In two respects, however, Lewisporte led the way: first, by trying to take advantage of all the educational resources available; and second, by treating girls and young women on an equal basis with the boys and young men. In most of the small schools of Newfoundland, too, the children left the schools when they had reached physical maturity, irrespective of whether they had the option of carrying on. That was not the pattern in Lewisporte. Early in the life of the community, girls remained in school so long as teachers were able to teach them, and many of them had later opportunities for more education in places such as Toronto or New York.

Besides the schools, the other dominant aspect of Newfoundland's community life was the churches. Lewisporte, from its settlement in 1876 to the post-World War II social revolution, was a one-religion town except for a small but vigorous Salvation Army minority. Most of those who settled there were either Methodist (United Church) or married into a Methodist family. My father, Eli Rowe, and my uncle, Nathaniel Turner, were both Anglicans when they attended the Society (Anglican) School in Seldom. But when they came to Burnt Bay there was no Anglican clergyman or teacher, and since they eventually married the Methodist daughters of James Freake, they in time became identified with the Methodist Church — though at no time did my father repudiate his Anglican connection.

In a sense the church was big business, for it involved committees (finance, trustees, educational, etc.) and required help in organizing its various programs.

These activities give a good indication of how the work was carried on. Starting with Sunday, there were the regular services, an early morning service and an evening service followed by an "after-service" where the "converted" were expected to remain behind for hymn-singing and prayer. Sunday afternoon had two groups registered; the older group, the Bible Class, studied Scripture, and the younger group attended a Sunday school. It is worth noting that Lewisporte had one of the biggest Sunday schools of its kind in Newfoundland. My recollection is that among the Methodist and United Churches, it was second only to the one at Gower Street Church in St. John's.

The Sunday school, which of course I attended, was very well organized. All grades subscribed to literature at various levels, using texts supplied by the Ryerson Press of Toronto, a printing and publishing firm which, I understand, was at one time the largest in Canada. We studied the literature in much the same way as we did in day school. This gave me a tremendous advantage, since it was precisely in literary subjects that I excelled. Had the studies been in the field of mathematics and related subjects I would have been the class dunce, but with Biblical history I could walk away with anything set before me.

I recall that the first year the competitive examinations were given I wrote the answers down without much trouble. The results were made known later in the summer on a hot Sunday afternoon, and lo! like Abou Ben Adhem, I led all the rest as far as Lewisporte was concerned, and in all Newfoundland I was second. As I indicated earlier the Sunday school was large and there was some confusion about where to find me. Finally, one of my classmates admitted that while on the way to school he had seen Fred Rowe diving off the captain's bridge of the S.S. *Clyde*, one of the coastal boats. As I recall, there was no prize for me, but I still have the simple certificate showing that I had made 91 percent.

I feel that sufficient tribute has never been paid to the churches for their provision of good reading material, even if the material was at times restricted and partisan in nature. One of the periodicals supplied by the Ryerson Press was *The Onward*. It was really a religious magazine, folded into four sheets, that carried a feature story, a serial (after 60-odd years I still remember one called "Lost in the Northern Wilds"), a biblical "lesson," and news column. Older adults subscribed to or were given more advanced material, a practice still followed by the United Church of Canada, whose church-wide publication *The Observer* has received national commendation.

Since most of the residents were able to read and write, it is not surprising that quite a number subscribed to this or that publication. Another factor was that, after the branch railway was built in 1901, a number of the railway employees found the going pretty lonesome. In time the practice developed among them of buying popular novel sets, usually of ten or twelve books, that could be paid for over a period. Since as I grew older in the 1920s many of these temporary workers and I became friends, it was not long before I was taking advantage of their generosity. Thus I became familiar with the works of Zane Grey, James Oliver Curwood, Frank L. Packard, Rafael Sabatini, Ralph Connors, and Joseph Hocking.

Another source of reading matter was the gifts of relatives and friends who had left Lewisporte to settle in Toronto or New York. My mother's sister had seven daughters who reached adulthood, and of these only one remained in Newfoundland: four went to New York, and two went to Toronto. The daughters were most dutiful, and did not fail to send gifts periodically, a goodly portion of which consisted of books for their father. In the case of both my brother and me, quite literally the first books we ever read were Christmas gifts from our sister who had gone to Toronto to live.

An outstanding characteristic of our village was the emphasis placed on education, which was partly due to the Wesleyan tradition and partly due to the ties with Canada, especially Toronto.

In the 1890s, a Newfoundland-wide system of annual external testing was devised, to encourage competition and measure academic achievement. These examinations, based usually on prescribed textbooks, became enormously popular. Throughout Newfoundland, thousands of children and even whole classrooms competed with one another. Lewisporte prided itself on its good standing in these tests. This was brought about in part by the excellent attendance records in the schools. Also, possibly because of its relatively easy connection with the rest of Newfoundland by coastal boat and railway, Lewisporte did not suffer difficulty in recruiting good teachers to the extent that a great many other places did.

But it was more than school attendance and good teachers that kept standards high in Lewisporte. In 1922, with the proceeds from a school concert, the principal bought portions of two famous "libraries," the Nelson and J. M. Dent book series. These, of course, were editions of the classics which had done much to make Britain literate and civilized. At first not many in our school read these books, possibly because several tries had proved them a bit too tough. But, in time, Dickens, Scott, Ainsworth, and others found their devotees. I was nine or ten at the time, but I soon discovered that *Alice in Wonderland*, *Gulliver's Travels*, *Lorna Doone*, and *Robinson Crusoe* were suitable for all ages.

The circumstance that, more than anything else, gave me a chance to read hundreds of books at no cost to my family, was the fact that after my father had come ashore for good, he became manager of the general store in the west end founded by my mother's brother, Uriah Freake.

Uncle Uriah was an indefatigable worker, always ready to take risks; my father was in some ways the opposite—quiet, reserved, loyal. But together they made an unbeatable team.* As manager of the store and related business—a herring factory, a fox farm, a forge, and other enterprises—my father had a free hand in ordering, selling, and pricing. At the time there were no vehicles except for a horse and cart and a go-cart. But there were two means of transport besides walking to and from the two main stores, at least for mail and money: my brother and I, who acted as messengers. Any letter or parcel containing money had to be placed in Uncle Uriah's hands, and for this, we would normally be given something either in cash or in kind. The usual reward was five cents.

Such an errand gave us a chance to look around the big store, which had a number of features not to be found in the smaller establishment we called "our" store. One day, while taking advantage of my privileged status (after all, wasn't I the nephew of the great man who owned all these exotic things?) I noticed something new—books unlike those few which we sometimes had in stock.

For one thing, they had soft or paper covers instead of hard covers. And the covers looked different—beautiful women, and tall and athletic young men frequently rescuing the former from some terrible fate. Also, the prices were ridiculously low for the 1920s, only 20 cents new. Some of the characters' and writers' names were vaguely familiar: Buffalo Bill, Horatio Alger, Nick Carter. But one book was completely new to me, though not for

---

* Uncle Uriah died of cancer when he was only 45. My father carried on as before for about five years; then, with the onslaught of the Depression, the east-end business was sold, but my father continued to manage the west end for several years. He eventually went into business for himself, but was felled by a massive stroke in 1936.

long: Burt L. Stanish was the writer and the title carried Frank Merriwell's name.

As I looked over these books my excitement knew no bounds. If Uncle Uriah could have these for sale, why couldn't my father? As soon as I reached "our" store I gave him the story, and got from my father a promise to order 20 copies of various types.

They soon arrived and in short order were sold out. But here was a problem. My interest in these books was that I wanted to read them myself, something obviously impossible if customers bought the books a few days after their arrival. For several weeks I pondered this and then — light. I went to my father and pointed out that he shouldn't be bothered with so little a matter as these three or four dozen books; rather, he should let me take on sole responsibility for arranging the display, ordering fresh copies in place of some of the repeats, and drawing customers' attention to this or that one that I had heard about. And all this out of the goodness of my heart — I would not expect to get paid.

I am quite sure my father saw through my scheme without any trouble; but if so, he was kind enough not to humiliate me. And so, when a shipment of Street and Smith's dime novels arrived from Dicks and Company, I took over. After due examination I placed on display all those that I had read — or those that I had no intention of reading such as Ethel M. Dell, Mrs. Signorary, etc., books about silly men and women falling in love and getting mixed up in all kinds of troubles.

I thought, how could anyone bother with that balderdash when Frank Merriwell was there waiting? Without any doubt Frank was the world's greatest athlete. He excelled in every sport known to man, and he always came out on top in spite of overwhelming odds. Accompanying him, as part of his coterie, were a group whose loyalty could always be counted on. True, most of them had previously been his enemies, but their hostility had been overcome by Frank's generosity and concern; most owed their lives to him. With him, too, were Elsie and Inza, one blonde and the other brunette, both in love with Frank but never willing to let it be known.

I read the entire Merriwell series, around 220 books in all. Then there was the Buffalo Bill series. No football or baseball here — nothing but that great unrelenting West. And if that proves dull, what about Nick Carter? Only concern for the great Sherlock's most sensitive feelings kept Nick's army of followers from proclaiming their hero's superiority to the world.

How many did I read? All of them. Every book in every series: Buffalo Bill, with over 100 titles; Horatio Alger, with over 200; Nick Carter, with over 100. Did they hurt me? No. Did I derive benefit? Yes.

I have left out the most popular periodical that Newfoundland ever enjoyed, the *Family Herald and Weekly Star*, a farming publication. I have been told that no paper or magazine has ever been able to stand up against it — a rather strange fact, since its very nature would seem not to recommend it in a land where farming was so little practised. Actually, I have a feeling that the farmers of Newfoundland may have used the paper more than they let on. Whatever the reasons, no other publication exceeded it in circulation. My father subscribed to it when he was 20 years old.

I seem to remember that the charge was one dollar and 50 cents a year, or perhaps it was only a dollar. The *Family Herald* was a big periodical, and, as I recall (some 65 years later), it had separate sections for just about every department of the paper. Some of the departmental names were meaningless to me, e.g. "Horticulture," but not so the weekly articles by Churchill, Mussolini, and Lloyd George; and not so the column known as "The Observer," which was the first part of the paper my father tried to get out of mother's hands on Saturday night.

Weekly, one whole page of the *Family Herald* was devoted to the Maple Leaf Club. My guess is that the Club did more than any other single thing to put the maple leaf on our national flag. And it certainly did much to instill in children a desire to maintain the British connection.

2 The Development of Lewisporte

*A*fter basic food supplies, the Newfoundland settlers had one great necessity—wood. First of all, lumber was needed to build a house and adjoining sheds. Then, firewood was needed, as well as lumber and logs for stages, wharves, and, of course, boats. But if settlers were going to remain settlers, they also had to be near their basic food supplies—codfish, caplin, salmon, herring, seal meat, and sea birds—all of which were in or near the ocean and, as settlement continued, farther and farther away from the sources of wood.

Clearly, some compromise had to be reached. That compromise, which probably started in Trinity Bay and in time spread to most parts of Newfoundland, consisted of having a permanent summer residence near the fish and water communications, but using the schooners, skiffs, and other boats to take fishery sup-

plies from the coast in to the bottoms of the bays, where there was
plenty of wood and where other, supplementary food was available (in the form of, for example, caribou, beaver, and, after
their introduction around the middle of the last century, rabbits).
Of course, a cabin or tilt of logs and moss had to be built to
shelter the family for the winter; but shelter was not a serious
problem, since the tilt would be surrounded by the forest.

During the winter, trees were cut for fuel and for sawing into
lumber by using pit saws (long saws). A pit saw required two men
and had the added disadvantage of being hazardous, but it
enabled the sawing of the very large pine, spruce, and fir that
were needed for schooners and other construction. When the ice
had moved off in the spring, preparations were made to return to
the coast to get ready for the fishing.

Not everyone adopted these procedures. In many communities
wood supplies were near enough to the coast to enable the settlers
to enjoy the best of both worlds. There would be sealing in the
spring, fishing in the summer, shooting birds and other hunting
in the fall, and trapping beaver, foxes, weasels, and lynx in the
winter. While the men were in the woods, they usually left the
family at home. One disadvantage of this practice was that the
tasks of carrying water, sawing and cleaving wood, and perform-
ing the hundreds of physical chores that maintained a measure of
cleanliness and respectability had to be done by the women.

At this point, a concise study of Lewisporte itself would be both
interesting and useful. As it happens, its history can be divided
into three parts: a primitive period from 1875 to around 1900, a
second, industrial period from around the turn of the century
until 1939, and a third period from the beginning of World War
II on, which may be termed the modern period.

The first period saw the transition from log huts to well-built
wooden houses, each surrounded by cleared land, and the establishment of a church and a school (initially one building) to meet
the demands of the several hundred inhabitants who were gradually making Lewisporte one of the larger communities in Notre
Dame Bay. But in spite of the obvious progress and growth,
Lewisporte was still cut off from contact with the outside, even
more so than were Fogo and Twillingate, which at least were still
among the chief ports of call for the hundreds of schooners going
back and forth to the Labrador.

There was one important difference between Lewisporte and
the great majority of other settlements during the period. As

in the case of the other settlements, Lewisporte men still went to the Labrador, shipping out usually on the boats belonging to the great fishing companies of Notre Dame Bay such as the Hodges, the Earles, the Ashbournes, and the Manuels. (My father, who shipped with Duder for several summers, once told me that the firm sent more than 200 vessels to the Labrador, and that when he sailed with the Manuels, Josiah Manuel personally owned 21 schooners.) But by the 1890s, Lewisporte was no longer a one-industry town.

The men who lived in Seldom or Moretons Harbour had only one occupation: the fishery. Their economic life revolved around it in one form or another; if the fishery failed, and if the supply merchant was unable or unwilling to extend further credit, hunger and eventual starvation confronted them. If the fish merchants were plagued by lack of fish, bad markets, or ice blockages, most of them faced ultimate bankruptcy, contrary to the age-old myth among Newfoundlanders regarding the wealth they possessed.

Obviously, if a place were fortunate enough to have two or more industries, especially if those industries experienced year after year of good fortune, prosperity was likely. Thus Lewisporte, with its magnificent harbour, one of the best in Canada, and with its great stretches of nearby timber ideal for boat and schooner building and for lumber generally, could look forward to a bright future. That feeling was shared not only by the people, but also by Sir Robert Bond, the prime minister of Newfoundland from 1900 to 1913 and Member for the district of Twilligate, who stated while being rowed across Lewisporte Harbour by my father and uncle: "If God ever meant any place in Newfoundland to be a city it is Lewisporte."* Certainly, by the end of the century, while Lewisporte was far from being a city, the people were not only fishing but logging and farming as well. Indeed, some had given up their fishing to devote themselves full-time to the other two industries.

But around the turn of the century, Lewisporte was to have a plethora of job opportunities. The railway from St. John's to Port aux Basques had been completed, and soon work was under way to build the branch to Lewisporte. This job became all the more urgent as news of another great enterprise spread around: this

---

* Both my father and my uncle, separately, attributed the quotation as given above to Bond, a man famous for his moderation.

was the establishment of the greatest sawmilling operation in Newfoundland's history, a project that would utilize the pine forests of the interior, specifically at Glenwood on the Gander River and at Red Indian Lake on the Exploits River. Cutting down the trees was, of course, only part of the operation. The logs had to be transported, sawn, and shipped, and the place selected for this mighty operation was Lewisporte; the piers and lumberyard that were built for this purpose were the largest in Newfoundland.

One of the significant results of the railway and sawmill operations was that the great majority of the labourers had their first contact with actual cash. The men were paid one dollar a day—a very satisfactory rate indeed—and this was paid to each individual worker, with no middlemen. Clearly, for the people of Lewisporte, fishing was likely to have to take second place. Not only were the labourers to enjoy the work of constructing the railway and the lumbering installations, but for many of them there would be opportunities for permanent employment, especially with the railway.

With the completion of the branch to Lewisporte, a coastal service could be introduced. The ships for this service were the "alphabet" fleet: *Argyle*, *Bruce*, *Clyde*, *Dundee*, *Ethie*, *Fife*, *Glencoe*, and *Home*. The ships allocated to Notre Dame Bay were *Clyde* and *Home*, both of which were destined to have a distinguished record in the Newfoundland coastal service. The two ships each had a crew of 21, some of whom lived at Lewisporte. The service called for wharfingers who were responsible for coaling, transferring freight, and servicing the ships in other ways as they got ready for their weekly or biweekly trips. On the railway side, the crew on the Lewisporte branch were all stationed in Lewisporte, as were the section men who kept the lines in good repair. This coastal and branch railway service not only gave permanent jobs to perhaps 20 or more Lewisporte men, but from time to time gave temporary work to scores of men. Thus the railway and the steamship lines were new industries.

By the end of the century, with the population now over 300, a number of settlers had turned to full-scale farming and the majority of the others were using part-time farming to supplement their income from other sources. As this reliance on farming and logging increased there was a corresponding decline in the reliance on fisheries. One indication of this is the fact that, in my whole life up to the time that I was a teenager, I had seen only one lobster, and the codfish that my father carried for sale in the store came from Joe Batts Arm and Fogo, the very places earlier Lewisporte settlers had partly forsaken to get away from fishing.

Early in this century, another great development affecting Lewisporte was the decision by certain British money interests to produce electricity using the water power of the Exploits River, the largest river on the Island of Newfoundland, and to use the power and the Newfoundland forests to manufacture pulp and paper. The mill site chosen for the operation was Grand Falls, about ten miles west of the railway centre of Bishops Falls. The people of Lewisporte strongly hoped that the Anglo-Newfoundland Development Company would do as Lewis Miller had done several years earlier, utilize Lewisporte's great harbour and the branch railway to make the settlement a shipping port for the thousands of tons of paper that would have to be exported.

Unfortunately from Lewisporte's point of view, after debating the matter at some length Anglo-Newfoundland Development settled on Botwood. One reason suggested by some to explain the decision was that if Lewisporte were chosen the company would be in the hands of the Reid Newfoundland Company, which owned and controlled the Lewisporte branch, whereas by building a new branch to run from Grand Falls to Botwood the company would be the master of its own house. A much stronger reason, perhaps, was that from the mill site in Grand Falls to the sea in Botwood the distance was only 20 miles, while from the mill site to Lewisporte the distance was about 40 miles.

Thus, with the implementation of the railway program, with the Miller project, short-lived though it was (he was bought out in 1903), and with increased forestry operations to feed the great mill at Grand Falls, Lewisporte had entered an industrial era. This second phase, which, of course, included World War I, lasted until around 1938–1939. Even the world depression had less effect on Lewisporte than it did on the great majority of Newfoundland settlements. Many people (including my father) were victims of that economic decline, but it is true that for the most part Lewisporte's residents maintained a fair degree of prosperity. The railway and the coastal boats still ran; the paper mill still needed pulpwood; and because of the need to make train and ship connections going or coming, the half-dozen hotels and several restaurants flourished until 1938 or so, when the preparations for World War II started to dominate the picture.

During the first decade of the century, under Sir Robert Bond, and later, under Sir Edward Morris, Newfoundland made steady progress in road-building, farming, lumbering, and other aspects. Then there was the impetus given to the whole economy by the Grand Falls enterprise, and added to all this was the expansion of mining at Bell Island in Conception Bay. Within a year or so after the beginning of World War I, Lewisporte started to experience a phenomenon experienced only once before, a period of full-scale employment and relative prosperity.

This continued until the end of the war, but with the advent of peace it soon disappeared. In particular, the fisheries went sour and the markets declined. Early in the 1920s, firms were going broke all over Newfoundland. It is not my intention to write an economic history of Newfoundland, but it should be noted that each period of recession and depression was brought about by failure in one way or another of some aspect of the fisheries: weather, fish migration, markets, etc. Even the bankruptcy of 1931 and 1932 would not have shaken Newfoundland as fiercely as it did but for two successive fishery failures. By the same token, the periods of relative prosperity would not have occurred without fishery successes. The only exceptions to this generalization in modern times were due to the World Wars, which both created full employment for several years.

With the building of Gander Airport, linked to Lewisporte by train and later by highway as well, the town expanded into its third phase, which continues to the present. The most important factor in that development was the building of the mightiest fuel tanks in Newfoundland as literally thousands of aircraft converged on Gander to refuel in preparation for the critical crossing of the Atlantic. But by the end of World War II and the Cold War, the people of Gander and Lewisporte foresaw a serious decline as the great jets tended to bypass Gander. But that tendency was only temporary. Gander is still one of the most strategic airports in the world, and Gander and Lewisporte are still among the most prosperous towns in Newfoundland and Canada. In 1935, when I took up the census in Lewisporte, the population was 699; today it is about 4000. The idyllic village of the second phase is no more, but in its place is one of the best-planned towns in the province.

Lewisporte now depends, for the most part, on the airport some 30 miles away and on the great ferries linking up the Island of Newfoundland and the territory of Labrador, particularly Labrador's industrial complex created by Goose Airport and

Happy Valley. Much of Lewisporte's prosperity relates to these two great airports, which contributed so much to the Allied victory nearly 50 years ago, and which helped to make Lewisporte's third phase the most gratifying period of its entire history.

chapter
3 *Lewisporte in the 1920s*

I have chosen the Lewisporte of the 1920s as a Newfoundland village worthy of being analyzed and dissected, not because it was a typical Newfoundland community of that time, but rather because it was one of the small number that were not. There is, too, the obvious fact that it is one of the communities and periods that I know best: my parents were among the founders, and my contacts with the place remained strong until I left home permanently in 1936.

During that period the Newfoundland Railway was still very much a part of the economic life, as were, of course, the coastal boats and other boats, big and small, that took advantage of the beautiful harbour Sir Robert Bond had praised so much.

The Lewisporte residents of the 1920s were peaceful and law-abiding (we had one policeman), homogeneous, churchgoing, sober, provident, hard-working, and anxious to maintain appearances. A majority of the houses had gable roofs, two or two-and-a-half storeys, with four or more bedrooms, a dining room, and a parlour or sitting rrom, which last was rarely used and then only for very special occasions such as weddings and funerals. The most important room in the house, very often the largest and an adjunct to the rest of the house, was the back kitchen, which served usually as a dining, recreation, and general-purpose room. The back kitchen contained such things as a large wood-burning stove, a large table capable of accommodating eight or ten members of the family, a spinning wheel, a framed mat to be hooked according to a special pattern, cupboards containing dishes and preserves, a wood-box containing cloven wood and "splits," and a washstand with a basin. Very often there was another adjunct to the main house usually referred to as the back porch. This room had a barrel for drinking water, space to hang working clothes, space for supplementary wood in the winter-time, and room for tools and other implements. In addition to the house as described above, there were usually one or two out-houses: one, of course, was the discreetly located and euphemisti-cally termed "water closet"; the other would house any cattle or poultry and was usually referred to as the barn or stable.

Just about every house in Lewisporte was painted (usually white with green or grey trim), and with a few exceptions the house was on cleared land surrounded by a fence made of rails, pickets, or slabs. The fence served both to keep out marauding animals and to indicate where land boundaries were—the latter a not unim-portant function in Newfoundland, where land was so precious.

The average family in Lewisporte kept livestock and poultry (no dogs were then allowed in Lewisporte). Sometimes the live-stock consisted of a cow, for obvious reasons; often it was sheep for making wool (which was used to knit, among other things, almost all the winter clothes); and pigs and goats were common, in spite of the latter's destructive nature. Another animal fairly common in Lewisporte was the horse or pony. Both were particu-larly useful for collecting firewood, which as the town developed became increasingly hard to find. And once the winter snow had packed hard and smooth, the animal could be used for pleasure as well as utility. Ponies were also convenient when there was no other means of transportation. As for poultry, it provided not only eggs to eat, but also roasted birds for the Sunday dinner once in a while.

Lewisporte was near enough to the Grand Falls paper opera-tions to partake of some of the economic benefits. A number of the contractors were domiciled in Lewisporte and it was common for them to bring the huge horses they used to haul wood and logs to Lewisporte for care and fodder, thus adding another facet to our economic growth.

The residents of Lewisporte were almost entirely Methodist in religious practice, although before settling, some of them had been adherents of the Church of England. When a few of the Methodists branched off to become members of the Salvation Army, they received little encouragement from their friends. The Army's struggle for survival as a religious group in a community where the parent church was so entrenched was a long and difficult one. But as the years went by the Army became both stronger and more acceptable, to the point in fact where the two groups acted as one in many community matters.

Although it was a church recognized by the government for educational purposes, the Army did not always make use of its rights in this matter. My own feeling is that this was due as much to the failure of the Army people as it was to Methodist antagonism. Then, too, as matters stood Army children were welcomed into the Methodist schools, while if the Army insisted on its right to be treated as an independent educational body, it would probably create a situation where untrained teachers struggled with one small, all-grade school while the Methodists (United Church) enjoyed the benefits of a three-room school — at that time a fairly acceptable situation in education circles in Newfoundland. At no time did the Army build a school in Lewisporte. It is significant that when the movement towards amalgamated schools started to spread from company towns such as Grand Falls and Corner Brook, one of the first non-company towns to advocate a system of joint schools was Lewisporte.

The people of Lewisporte enjoyed more of a cash economy than the great majority of other villages in the 1920s did. Perhaps the explanation for this lay in its early history. The early settlers of Newfoundland, with nothing but an axe and saw, had to clear land, keep cattle, and grow crops just to stay alive. But in Lewisporte, with the advent of the Railway, the sawmills, and the cutting of pulpwood the need for subsistence farming had disappeared from some homes, at least until the Depression years.

In my boyhood home, my father, as manager of a store, received a monthly salary, and this plus the benefits of such a position meant that, while not wealthy, we were, by Newfoundland standards, reasonably comfortable. We enjoyed certain luxury items as a matter of routine—oranges and other fruit, bacon, ham, cheese, marmalade, packaged cereal, etc. But at no time did my mother overlook a basic possibility: that the relative luxuries provided by a good job in a store were at best ephemeral and could disappear almost overnight. In fact, in my father's case the combination of the prolonged effects of a stroke and a situation, a result of the depression, where customers were helpless to repay debts, once produced almost exactly such a crisis, which was warded off only by the dedicated efforts of other members of the family.

Early in his Lewisporte career my father applied for and received a government grant of 12 acres of land near the bottom of Lewisporte; there, he cleared a portion of the land, built a house, and grew grass and potatoes. But this house was "burnt" by a forest fire, so he took advantage of a piece of land from my grandfather's estate. It was not large, but it was suitable for the basic crops of potatoes, turnips, carrots, parsnips, and cabbage, and for the perennial crop of rhubarb and black and red currants that mother raised for preserves. This last crop was augmented by wild raspberries, blueberries, and, on occasion, partridge berries. Land not cultivated for our own nourishment was used to produce hay for the livestock; some of the hay was dried and stowed in the barn for winter use.

For many years we kept a cow, which supplied us with milk, cream, and butter, and which periodically produced a calf which, if it was a bull, could be slaughtered for food. Whenever for some reason we did not have a cow, we kept goats, which also produced milk and on occasion venison. For many years we kept sheep whose wool in time resulted in wool socks, sweaters, caps, scarves, and the like. The entire process, from shearing the sheep to covering one's head or body, was done in the house, usually by one person, my mother.

My mother insisted on keeping exactly a dozen hens (and one rooster). From time to time that number would be exceeded, but only until the birds had matured enough to be eaten for a Sunday dinner. Our chickens ensured us a steady supply of fresh eggs, and many others adopted my mother's system. Of course, a number of families, for one reason or another, were unable to; in such cases, charity often entered the picture, or, where this was not needed, we sold to the families, at modest prices, any surplus eggs. We also helped out with other produce.

Two things that we ourselves lacked, along with just about

everyone else, were a steady supply of clean water and electricity. One or two homes did have primitive indoor plumbing — pumps that brought water by suction from a well under the house — and one or two hotels did have a dynamo or generating system to give them some electrical power, usually on a very limited basis. But these were exceptions. In most houses, for example, illumination was provided by kerosene lights. These oil lamps were much less efficient than the Aladdin's lamp, itself temperamental, which became increasingly popular in the 1920s and 1930s.

Since most of the stoves were wood-burning, as a rule only the kitchen was heated, and that only during the daylight hours; the other stoves in the house were rarely in use, and if coal was used it was only for very special occasions. Because of the lack of central heating, running water was entirely out of the question, and because most of the houses did not have weatherproof basements, it was impossible to store water there in the winter. Thus, the majority had to depend on a brook or a community well for water. That in turn meant that there would be a critical shortage of water when the well or brook was subjected to particularly cold weather. Apart from St. John's, a few of the largest towns such as Harbour Grace, and the company towns, there was no community water supply. Very often the water had to be brought long distances, either in buckets or in barrels on carts or sleighs, and since the men were frequently away from home the drudgery had to rest quite literally on the shoulders of the women.

But life was not all drudgery or boredom in the Lewisporte of the first third of this century. There was some sport and recreation, especially among the male teenagers. Once in a while the harbour became a glistening three miles of glass, and then it was fascinating to see how many pairs of skates could be resurrected. Most of the boys and some of the girls knew how to swim by the time they were 12 or 13, and strange as it seems, much of the swimming was done in the harbour rather than in the freshwater pond nearby. I was only 16 when I fulfilled a long-cherished dream of swimming nonstop across the Lewisporte bay.

The great sport of Lewisporte, however, was not swimming or skating, but soccer, which we called "football." When we played the game we laboured under great difficulty: there was for many years no real field on which to play, and where there was a block of ground, the rocks or holes or stumps made the undertaking perilous; as if this were not enough, the cows, horses, and sheep could be relied on to make life miserable for all but the most nimble. But play we did. Because of its location, Lewisporte was a port of call for many English cargo ships and from time to time British warships as well. I do not recall ever losing a game to the English and Norwegian visitors. And invariably, they congratulated us and expressed their amazement that a comparative village could turn out a team that held its own against former Arsenal players.

Nor was the social program confined to young men. For most of the time dancing was forbidden, since it was one of the activities that the old Wesleyan Church had frowned on, the others being cardplaying and drinking alcohol. But it was easy to modify the old steps—the square dances, lancers, etc.—in such a way that they were only "games" known as "The Grand Old Duke of York" or "There Was a Johnny Miller." Besides the "socials," the schools or the church or community organizations always produced at least one play a year, usually a melodrama. And Christmas brought the mummers and the carols.

More sedentary, but no less exciting, were the card games played not with the ordinary playing cards that we use today for poker, but a modified type whose appearance was a concession to the Methodist suspicion that playing cards had to be watched. This suspicion was also reflected in the games themselves, which had names like "Flinch" and "Rook."

I referred earlier to the custom Lewisporte people had of painting their fences and the outside of their houses and smaller buildings. This beautification of the outdoor environment was complemented by keeping potted flowers indoors on a year-round basis. Today, reference to the practice almost invariably raises eyebrows or leads to skeptical questions, since everyone knows that houses then had no all-night heat and the cold in winter was almost unbearable. But the people of Lewisporte, and no doubt of other places, had devised a procedure to make winter house flowers possible.

In my mother's case, she had importuned my father to build her a rather strong box which was then made almost frostproof by building a second box around it, leaving a generous air space between. This box-within-a-box was then covered with mats and old clothing. It was kept fairly near to the kitchen stove, which would be giving off heat from about 7 a.m. to 11 p.m. The empty box would be absorbing heat all day. The result of all this was that before going to bed my mother or one of the family could place the flowers in the box and they would remain safe and warm through the night. As soon as my mother was up and around and the kitchen had heated up, she would open the box and place the flowerpots on windowsills and tables as near to light as possible — representing another victory over a hostile environment.

Today, at our country place at Lawrence Pond, where we have been cultivating trees since we first acquired wilderness land almost 40 years ago, we have, as far as we can ascertain, at least one specimen of every Newfoundland tree species. When I stroll through these magnificent pines, spruces, etc., I never cease to experience profound happiness. But honesty compels me to say that the greatest joy of all comes when I stop by the land in Lewisporte where our old house used to be and still see there the balsam, poplar, and dogberry trees that my brother Harold and I helped our mother to transplant over 60 years ago.

As I indicated earlier, my grandfather, James Freake, was one of the first settlers in the bay, a fact reflected in the quality of the land granted to him by the government. By contrast, the original settlers were unfortunate in the type of land they acquired for a church and related facilities. So when the original church was abandoned, these people decided to approach James Freake's heirs to see whether a suitable piece of land might be bought. This was arranged by Uriah Freake, my mother's brother. The block (120 by 90 feet) was sold to the church for $50.

Such transactions were possible because only part of the land had been cleared for houses and crops. Earlier, when suitable cemetary land was becoming scarce, my grandfather had made available a block of his land for burial purposes. It is of some interest to note that he was buried on that block, as were several others of the Freake family. It was particularly pleasing to us that when Mother died in St. John's and we took her body to Lewisporte to lie next to Father, the minister, Rev. A. B. Legrow, suggested that the casket be placed in the anteroom of this same church for the night preceding her burial. That night, her body was resting on land that she and her two sisters had helped to clear with their own hands. A short while later, we were very happy to be able to donate one of the two beautiful stained-glass windows now gracing the new church. This was a fitting tribute to a couple that had supported the church in so many ways.

The new church was completed in 1916 and remained in use until 1964. It too was built on land that had once belonged to my grandfather; the site is still one of the best in Lewisporte, overlooking as it does the matchless harbour and a rolling countryside. Both my father and my mother were buried from the above church and rest along with other members of our family in the old cemetery. My father died July 24, 1944 and my mother August 29, 1961.

The Freakes had worked and suffered for their religion, which is another way of saying that they did not take their religion lightly. Since during the 19th century the Methodists had increased in numbers and influence to the point where by the turn of the century they dominated eastern Newfoundland and Notre Dame Bay, it is worth making a study of one of them. For this purpose, again, I can do no better than to select my own mother, Phoebe Ann Freake.

A Wesleyan Methodist, she held certain beliefs that it was idle for anyone to try to shake. First of all, there was religion. She knew there was a God; she knew that everyone had to answer for his or her conduct. These fundamental beliefs were part of her very nature, and while the fact that her children might turn out to be agnostics or even atheists undoubtedly grieved her, it had no more effect on her beliefs than a summer shower.

She went to church every Sunday evening. (Sunday morning was reserved for preparing the dinner, which was eaten at 1 p.m.) On Sunday afternoon when her children were in Sunday school, she went to the Bible class, a session devoted to singing, testimony, prayers, and some religious instruction. She belonged to several women's groups within the church, notably the Women's Missionary Society—"the W.M.S."—which she supported both financially and psychologically. I never ceased to wonder at the temperament of a woman whose conscience compelled her, sometimes in spite of her own straitened circumstances, to contribute from her feeble resources money and time to help send missionaries to India, China, and Japan.

Mother worked from seven in the morning to eleven at night. One reason for these barbarous hours was her devotion to some of Wesley's other principles, in this case the Wesleyan dictum that cleanliness is next to godliness. This cleanliness was not only personal, of course. It meant all of us had to change clothes regularly; equally, it meant scrubbing the floor and polishing the wood stove every Saturday.

As in early Lewisporte, during the 1920s education continued to be an important part of the Methodist tradition and the community. Wesley himself was a highly educated man, considered by some non-Wesleyans to be one of the most highly educated men in England. This may have accounted for the emphasis he placed on education. Whatever the cause, Wesley supported education for his entire life and this tradition carried on after Wesley's death, becoming an integral part of the Wesleyan doctrine. In Newfoundland there were periods when even one-, two-, or three-room Methodist schools showed disproportionately high achievements at all educational levels, especially in higher and postgraduate studies. This disproportion was also manifested periodically in the annual number of matriculants and university graduates.

In Lewisporte there was almost continuous pressure on pupils to achieve good records in both attendance and studies. For decades, when the average attendance in Newfoundland was little better than 50 percent, Lewisporte had nearly 100 percent attendance after allowing for illness.

Mother had a very effective way of dealing with the problem of truancy. Number one: It was no use for the offender to expect to be allowed to help in such things as picking berries and digging potatoes; and chances were that neighbours' mothers would apply the same sanctions to the truant. If the excuse given for not going to school was sickness of any kind, then there was one pretty certain method: "bed until better." When a healthy boy pretends illness and then has to toss around for several hours in bed, he is likely to see the activities of school in a more welcome light.

Sexual morality was another ever-present reminder of Wesley and his philosophy. Except in the context of actual or imminent marriage, every possible measure was taken to protect girls from the more aggressive males. If a taboo within the framework of marriage was broken by a married woman and the fact became known, she could expect ostracism for years into the future. One reason for the adamant attitude of wives regarding adultery was the fact that, when adultery did take place, the husband was usually away engaging in some of the world's most hazardous occupations: sealing, fishing, or logging. That a wife would betray her husband under such circumstances was beyond comprehension.

My mother's response to one woman who did just that illustrates what an unfaithful wife could expect: A husband who was away from home for some six or seven months returned home to become the recipient of unwelcome news. He walked out of his house and out of Lewisporte. A few days later the woman was in my father's store shopping when my mother entered. When the woman greeted my mother in a normal way, mother looked through her as if the woman did not exist. At the time, the rest of us thought such treatment too harsh, but to my mother's mind there was no excuse for the woman's conduct. The offence was unpardonable, and even our appeal to Wesley's doctrine of charity failed to change her mind. Her attitude was shared by the great majority of the women in Lewisporte and, for that matter, the women of most of the Lewisportes of Newfoundland. Black was black, white was white, and that was that!

My father was in some ways the antithesis of my mother. Where she was assertive he was reticent; where she would not hesitate to express her views he inclined towards moderation. But on fundamental issues they thought alike and their unalterable affection for each other was evident to all. Here, too, Mother was never backward in expressing herself. Though some of her convictions did not go beyond her wifely duties, in society she knew that her husband was right and she was ready to fight anyone who might insinuate otherwise. Here again, an incident in the store, which took place when I was eleven or twelve, is revealing.

Jim Johnson (to use a name not extant in Lewisporte) was in the lumber woods cutting pulpwood for one of the contractors. Like many other cutters, from time to time Jim got a small advance on his potential, usually five or ten dollars, and sent it home in an envelope. Larger amounts would be registered or sent as a money order. One morning, Jim's wife, Mary, arrived at the store a minute or two after Father had unlocked the door. It was clear that she had received a little money from Jim. She ordered several items, for which she tendered all she had, a five-dollar bill. Father gave her the small amount of change left over and she left for home, which was about a quarter of a mile away. A few minutes later I looked out the window to see Mary approaching with a very determined look on her face. As I watched, she came in and without any preliminaries attacked my father orally, alleging that she had given him a ten-dollar bill, not a five. Father, who remembered the transaction, protested, quite mildly as usual, that it had been only five dollars. Nevertheless, he opened the cash register to convince himself, and both he and I could see there was no ten-dollar bill in the register. This, of course, was no proof to Mary, and father's simple declaration of innocence only infuriated her the more.

The whole matter was explained, and made more difficult, by the simple fact that Mary, a relative newcomer to Lewisporte, could neither read nor write and, as we knew from experience, could not even recognize her own name on a cheque. Finally my father told her that if, when her husband came out of the woods, he confirmed that the bill was a ten, he would give her the other five. This did little to placate her, but it was clear that my father would not budge further and so she went home. Her husband came home about a month later. His first action was to go up to my father to apologize for his wife's behaviour. He said, "You know, she still doesn't know the difference between a five- and a ten-dollar bill."

Now, when the altercation occurred I went in to our house to tell my mother. She was most indignant that an illiterate such as Mary Johnson would dare talk in such a way to her blameless husband. So she did something that was unusual for her: advised her husband on a matter that concerned the business. "Eli," she said, "why didn't you open the door and tell her to get out?" Father hesitated for a few seconds, then sighed and, half-seriously, threw the ball to her: "Maid," he said, using his favourite term of affection for her, "what can you do with a fool?"

During most of its history, Lewisporte, like all but a few towns, lacked facilities for both medical and nursing attention. At first, this was taken in stride. People, young and old, got sick, and if it was a disease such as "decline" (tuberculosis), "inflammation of the bowel" (acute appendicitis), "stomach growth" (cancer), "infantile paralysis" (polio), or "inflammation of the brain" (spinal meningitis), we accepted death as almost inevitable. For adults pneumonia was always waiting on the sidelines to join up with measles, influenza, or one of the other acute diseases—ready on short notice to administer the final blow. The fatal arithmetic for pneumonia was almost exactly 50 percent. But what became difficult to accept were the many childhood diseases which were often a sentence of death: diphtheria, smallpox, rheumatic fever, whooping cough, croup, measles, the mumps. Some of these, if they did not kill, could deform and mutilate: the measles victim could be left blind or deaf; rheumatic fever most probably left the victim with a damaged and weakened heart. Worst of all, the infant killer, enteritis, waited to pounce, while the mother and her neighbouring friends watched in complete helplessness as the burning fever unremittingly mounted.

My mother's first child appeared healthy enough, but was dead within a few months from enteritis ("summer complaint"). Her first boy, by all accounts favoured of the gods, also picked up enteritis, and died a few days after being stricken; he was less than four years old. The youngest of her four girls became a victim of diphtheria; she lived only four days, by which time her heart had given out. Ironically, she was the only fatality in what was a rather moderate epidemic. After the epidemic had subsided, the government did send a doctor to Lewisporte to inoculate the entire population; but for one it was too late. The death of my ten-year-old sister was the heaviest blow we had experienced; and our bitterness was the greater because our two older sisters had gone to live in Toronto, and that baby sister was quite obviously the last of the family.

Moreover, we knew she should not have died. The entire population of Newfoundland had been vaccinated against smallpox a few years before, and everyone had known how vicious diphtheria could be; thousands of tombstones attested to this fact. Yet year after year had gone by without any action on the part of the various governments. The doctor only visited Lewisporte to administer the necessary injections a couple of weeks after my sister's death. The death of this ten-year-old girl shocked the Lewisporte-Grand Falls area, and may have been the cause for the government's unusual speed.

Of course, by then Sir Wilfred Grenfell had been working for years looking after the medical needs of many people in both Newfoundland and Labrador. My older sister, Ethel, born in the early 1900s, had been sickly and gave the impression she was not to live very long. Nevertheless, my mother exhibited her usual indomitable spirit and arranged somehow to take the child to St. Anthony, where the great Dr. Grenfell was ministering to the sick and disabled. He kept my sister in the hospital for about three weeks and then sent her back to Lewisporte, accompanied of course by my mother. Ethel eventually recovered.*

Even earlier, my father had had reason to be grateful for Grenfell's attention. As a Labrador fisherman and captain he had been exposed to a common ailment that was always serious and that with no medical attention sometimes led to death. This was an infection of the hands and wrists, probably the result of the unsanitary conditions under which these seamen lived and worked. When my father became infected he knew that his

---

* Dr. Grenfell's final word to my mother was that Ethel, then about 14, had tuberculosis of the bowels and could not live longer than a few weeks at most. But even from Grenfell himself my mother refused to accept such a verdict. Ethel is still living in Toronto, aged 86.

chances of complete recovery were remote, and that the possibility of fatal blood poisoning, which had killed his father, was
always present. As his condition grew worse my father recognized
that his hopes of survival were diminishing.

By chance, however, one of the schooners sailing south on
the Labrador coast reported having heard of the presence of the
famous doctor. Accordingly, with only sails and oars to rely on,
my father forced his schooner north as fast as he could. To his
great satisfaction, Dr. Grenfell's ship was located, and my father
lost no time in seeking out the Doctor himself. It took several
weeks for the infection to be brought completely under control,
but with surgery and disinfection victory resulted. My father
never ceased to be grateful to Grenfell, knowing from his long
experience that without Grenfell's ministrations his name might
well have become another Labrador statistic.

chapter
4 *The Rowe Family*

I have no doubt that some readers of this book will have no particular interest in the content of this chapter. On the other hand, since Rowes have now spread all over the English-speaking world (witness the number of entries in any telephone directory of a large community in, say, the United States), it stands to reason that thousands bear the name and therefore might be interested in the genealogy and history of this family. I suggest that those who have no special interest in the Rowe family simply pass on to more objective parts of the book.

It is obvious that most people are interested in their family background; it is equally obvious that few persons so interested have the ability and the resources to carry out meaningful genealogical research. Fortunately, that has not been the case with the Rowes. Both in Britain and in the United States, to name only two national groups, knowledge about this family has increased with the years. The researcher to whom Rowes are most indebted is undoubtedly Kenneth Allyn Rowe.

Kenneth Rowe was descended from John Rowe, the first settler of East Gloucester, Massachusetts, in 1651. John Rowe was born in Tavistock, southern England. Nobody knows when the first Rowes settled in England, but it was almost certainly before the year 1000 that Vikings, of whom the Rowes were part, conquered and settled in Normandy. One of the Breton Rowes sent four sons to accompany William the Conqueror when he invaded and conquered England in 1066. In 1190, according to Kenneth, Sir Everard Rowe was with Richard on the Third Crusade and was knighted by King Richard for his services. It is interesting to note that in his *Lives of the Poets*, Dr. Samuel Johnson devotes a lengthy chapter to Nicholas Rowe, poet laureate of England, in which he says that Nicholas was born just outside London where his West Country parents were temporarily domiciled.

The Rowes were particularly prominent during Elizabeth's reign. Three of them became Lord Mayor of London — Sir Thomas in 1568, Sir William in 1592, and Sir Henry in 1607. Earlier in the 1500s and going back to the 1400s, the Rowes were involved in municipal affairs, repeatedly rising to the rank of mayor. Richard was Mayor of Dartmouth in 1420, and his son William became Mayor of Totnes in Devon five times. Richard was also Provost of Bideford in 1417, while another Sir John was Sheriff of Cornwall in 1630.

Probably the most outstanding of the Rowe family were yet to come. Sir Thomas Rowe, a well-known explorer, was a friend of Sir Walter Raleigh. While in prison, Raleigh arranged with Rowe to lead an expedition to the Orinoco and Amazon Rivers to search for the gold that Raleigh was so sure was there waiting to be found. Rowe found no gold and Raleigh subsequently lost his head. Rowe's failure to secure gold did not interfere with his popularity as ambassador to India, Turkey, and Sweden. In fact, Emperor Gustavus Adolphus went on record as considering him the greatest ambassador he had ever seen.

Owen Rowe led an even more adventurous life than Sir Thomas. With the outbreak of the civil war in the 1640s, Rowe threw in his lot with Cromwell and by 1646 had become a colonel in Cromwell's army. When Charles's trial was finished, Rowe was one of the group who signed the death warrant. But with the restoration of Charles II to the throne the inevitable reprisals got under way. Rowe, who apparently was in bad health, asked for and was granted an audience with the King. Charles was not in-

clined to be vindictive, a fact that may explain his delay in signing Rowe's death warrant. Whatever the reason, Rowe escaped
the pending execution by simply dying and is buried under the
chapel in the Tower of London.

Nicholas Rowe's life was almost the antithesis of Owen's. Born
near London, of West Country descent, he took to law at an early
date, but his proclivity for literary and historical work soon
asserted itself. Several of his plays were the most popular of the
period: *The Fair Penitent* (where he coined the word "Lothario"),
Tamerlane, and *Jane Shore*. His Latin translations give him additional status, but his best claim to fame must be his 1709 edition
of Shakespeare, which in addition to providing what was, in
effect, the first biography of Shakespeare, divided the plays into
scenes and acts and supplied valuable textual material. Nicholas
Rowe died prematurely, at the age of 42, and was buried in Westminster Abbey in Poet's Corner next to the bust of Shakespeare.

The contributions the Rowes made to their country over a
period of years were considerable. The several branches of the
family were awarded at least 17 coats of arms. Of these perhaps
the best known are the Paschal Lambs and the one showing the
roebuck with what appears to be warriors readying for battle.
The latter was probably the one given to Nicholas Rowe's ancestor by Richard the First ("The Lion-Hearted").

The Rowes of England seem to have become more reticent in
the two centuries following Nicholas's death, but as reference to
the *Encyclopaedia Britannica* and, even more, the *Dictionary of
National Biography* shows, this can be misleading. The fact is
that they were spreading out from southern England to other
parts of the British Isles and to the various British colonies or
former colonies. As already pointed out, the author Kenneth
Rowe, whose Rowe research has been so valuable, was in direct
descent from the John Rowe who had settled in Massachusetts in
1651. There, however, life was not always peaceful, and when the
American Revolutionary War started John Rowe led his company
in the Battle of Bunker Hill, with the dedicated support of his
16-year-old son, also John Rowe. The family supported the
revolutionaries.

But the growing number of Rowe families did more than fight
battles. Many of their members became prominent theologians;
others became scholars of some renown; and others became connected with the West Country fisheries, whereby the merchants

outfitted ships that came out to Newfoundland in the early spring, caught a load of codfish, and returned to England in the fall. Since this fishery involved markets in the Mediterranean countries, the English ships frequently took their loads from Newfoundland, and after curing the fish carried it on to the markets around the Mediterranean Sea. Frequently the ships were able to bring back wines, tobacco, and other commodities to their homes in England, thus adding greater profit to the enterprise. As time went on, countries in the Caribbean area and South America became increasingly dependent on the Newfoundland fishery.

Settlement of the English and Irish in Newfoundland was subjected to adversity of one kind or another for most of the 17th century; this was usually due to war between England and France. On several occasions during the late 1600s and early 1700s, practically all English settlements on the English Shore (Cape Race to Cape Bonavista) were destroyed and the English and Irish settlers who had become domiciled in Newfoundland were shipped to France, eventually to become part of the exchange agreements between France and England. Most of these people had had their fill of Newfoundland life anyway, and did not return. Consequently the settlers who decided to go out to Newfoundland after the Treaty of Utrecht in 1714 were newcomers: the family names in 1730 bore little if any relationship to those to be found back in 1670.

Another factor complicating the picture was the lack of consistency in the fishery and migratory settlement. Frequently English and Irish fishermen remained in Newfoundland for several years and then when they met adverse conditions returned to England to join a ship going to Boston or Gloucester. To this day large numbers of Irish Americans trace their lineage to Newfoundland. In the early days of American colonization, New England interests encouraged the Newfoundland fishermen to abscond to the mainland. Those who did so often used illegal means to ignore the normal obligations; one was to change one's name, a device that may help to explain the periodic disappearance of some of the well-known Newfoundland names.

As with so many of the older Newfoundland families, no one can be sure of the actual date on which Rowe settlement first occurred, nor where it first occurred, What is beyond any doubt is that Rowes carried on an annual migratory fishery between the West Country of England (mostly Devon, Somerset, and Dorset) and Newfoundland, and that some time before 1750 Edward Rowe settled in the port of Trinity and was appointed a Justice of the Peace* or Magistrate for Trinity Bay. He carried out these duties until his death in 1754. All cases in the court were signed by Rowe and his fellow magistrate Thomas Warden, a practice that, I understand, was utilized by justices until comparatively recent times.

Apparently Edward Rowe, the magistrate, was the founder of the Rowes in Trinity Bay. They were shipbuilders and the port of Trinity was for a long time the most active and prosperous in the entire Bay.† But the Rowes soon found Trinity too restrictive for their activities.

Edward's wife and his son, James, were compelled to engage in a lawsuit that warranted the interference of the governor, who ruled in favour of James Rowe, a fact that may account for the subsequent expansion of the Rowe enterprise. Whatever the reason, the Rowes branched off to form another shipbuilding enterprise in Hearts Content on the southern side of the bay. Very soon activity on Rowe's "bank" (a geographical term for an area where the water is shallow) helped to make Hearts Content one of the most prosperous ports in the bay.‡

With two large shipbuilding enterprises turning out schooners at a fast clip, some of the Rowes settled permanently in Hearts Content. Others (including James, who eventually inherited the dynasty) periodically moved their families back and forth, with the result that some were listed as being born in Trinity and some in Hearts Content. Thus James's son Edward remained in Trinity, where he married Martha Pinhorn, who in 1806 produced a son, also Edward, my grandfather.

The Edward who became my grandfather married twice, but few details are known about his first wife; this is a pity, since all the present Rowes of Seldom-Come-By and hundreds who left to

---

* Care should be taken not to confuse the 1700s term "Justice of the Peace" with its modern use. The former were very real magistrates, with the power to administer fines and physical punishment whenever it was thought necessary.

† In 1753, when the Newfoundland census was taken, Magistrate Rowe had about 20 "servants" (fishers and fish processors) and "byeboat-keepers" (middlemen between coast fishermen and merchants). This probably meant that their shipbuilding enterprise was flourishing, since it would have been a heavy burden to keep so many at the fishery on a year-round basis. (See the Newfoundland archives.)

‡ Any reader interested in this part of Newfoundland's commercial history would do well to read Melvin Rowe's fascinating *I Have Touched the Greatest Ship* (St. John's, Nfld.: Town Crier Publishing Co., 1976).

seek their fortunes elsewhere are descended from that union. Edward Rowe's first wife died, leaving Edward with the responsibility of a family. As it happened, Captain Henry Osborne of
Seldom was lost at sea, leaving several children. So a double need
was met by the marriage of Edward Rowe, then the largest "fish-
killer" on Fogo Island, to Captain Osborne's widow, Mary Hale.*

The reader must have noticed that without any warning I have
switched from writing about the Rowes of Trinity and Hearts
Content to writing about the Rowes of Seldom-Come-By on Fogo
Island, over 100 miles to the north. As I mentioned earlier, Edward Rowe, my grandfather, was born in Trinity in 1806. But by
the early 1830s when he was married with several children, he was
living in Seldom. This raises the question as to why he migrated to
Fogo Island at a time when Trinity was apparently enjoying prosperous times.

Here we have to examine the economics and the physiography
of the fishing industry. To carry on a fishery, boats, nets, houses,
flakes, wharves, and stages are all required.† But above all, there
must be harbours, and a harbour is finite. It can accommodate
only so many boats at anchor. The foreshore can meet the spatial
needs, but only to a point. Likewise, there must be fishing
"banks" within a reasonable distance of the harbour. Once that
space is occupied there is no room for others. What can a 20-year-
old, anxious to set up his own premises, do in those circumstances? The answer in Trinity in the year 1800 was simply:
nothing. But for an enterprising entrepreneur there was one solution — go where there was unoccupied land and water, and this is
what Edward Rowe did. There could have been other factors
involved. The Fogo Island area has always been noted for the
richness of its fisheries, which is not surprising when one examines
its geography. Invariably, too, the island is surrounded by ice in
the spring and ice means seals.

Edward Rowe must have been familiar with these facts, either
from hearsay or by personal contacts while serving as a crew
member on his father's or some neighbour's schooner. It is inter-

---

* I have been unable to trace any information about Mary Hale's background in
  Cupids. It is possible she was there temporarily before her marriage to Captain
  Osborne. In any case my father always said his mother was born in Cupids and it is
  most unlikely that he would have erred in a matter of so much interest to him.

† *Flakes* are wooden structures, usually on stilts, with rails or slabs on which codfish is
  spread in order to effect drying by wind and sun. A *stage* is a combined wharf and
  housed-in structure for processing the fish — gutting, washing, salting, etc; usually
  the front of the stage is open.

esting to hear some of the legends, and possibly myths, retold about Rowe's arrival by Seldom inhabitants. One story, no doubt having some element of truth in it, is that at the time Seldom was populated by only one family, that of Holmes. When Edward Rowe's schooner came into the harbour and advised the leader of the Holmes family of his intention of settling on some of the land obviously not being used, it seemed like a bolt out of the blue. Holmes refused to concede, and for a time violence appeared likely. But this was averted in a time-honoured way: one of the Holmes girls fell in love with a husky handsome young Rowe. Her feelings were reciprocated, and so the two young lovers demanded that their elders forgo such nonsense as fighting when there was more important business at hand. How much of this legend is true? Certainly, there were marriages between the Holmeses and the Rowes, and the women are still famous for their beauty and the men for their drive and energy.

When I last visited Seldom three or four years ago, Victor Rowe, now deceased but then the patriarch of Seldom, took me to the point of land which had been agreed upon as the dividing mark between the two families. As I looked I could not help recalling how many men and women had gone on to further successes as a result of that fabled happy argument and union.

As the Rowes of Trinity declined in number, those in other villages, notably in Seldom but also in places in Trinity Bay such as Chance Cove and Green's Harbour, increased. The laying of trans-Atlantic cables in Hearts Content gave that community a high degree of prosperity and stability for many years. With other electronic developments, however, Hearts Content gradually declined, although evidence of its past glories still remained. The community became widely recognized for its export of professional people: doctors, engineers, clergymen, educators, businessmen, accountants, bank managers. Many of these came to St. John's but the large majority seem to have gone to Ontario and to the northeastern parts of the United States. My recollection is that when I came to St. John's in 1929 to go to school, the telephone directory contained only a small handful of Rowe listings, while today a rough calculation gives 115.

One interesting feature of the Rowe family is the degree of which physical resemblances are perpetuated. This has always been true of Newfoundland Rowes, even though most of them were unaware of it. When I was at Memorial in the 1930s one of my classmates was Duncan Rowe, later to become one of New-

foundland's best-known orthopedic surgeons.* When queried by
a third person about a possible relationship, each of us was careful to deny it, since Dunc was a Hearts Content Rowe and I was
from Lewisporte. Actually, as I later discovered, all we had to do
was to go back four generations to find a common ancestor in
James Rowe of Trinity and Hearts Content. Even I have had no
difficulty in detecting the resemblance between Dr. Bill Rowe,
dean of education at Memorial, and me, and between Melvin
Rowe, news director of the CBC for many years until his retirement, and me. While I am on this theme, it is interesting to note
the resemblance between Earl Rowe of Ontario and me. Though
we have never met, many of his friends have frequently accosted
me as being his younger brother, and sometimes his son. Earl was
one of the oldest parliamentarians in Canada, serving in Arthur
Meighan's and R. B. Bennett's cabinets, taking George Drew's
place as national leader of the Tory party when Drew's health
failed, and topping his honours with a term as Lieutenant Governor of Ontario. His daughter, Jean Wadd, who could have
passed as a twin of my sister, and who was herself a distinguished
political figure, served with great distinction as Canada's High
Commissioner at a time when the crucial constitutional talks between Canada and Britain were being held, talks which led to the
successful repatriation of our constitution.

It would seem most likely that one needs to go back only two or
three generations to get the Newfoundland connection. But, as
indicated by Prime Minister Wilson, physical traits can be carried
back longer periods. He was adamant that I closely resembled
some of the Rowes who were his friends in the West Country,
although I pointed out that there had to be a lapse of 200 to 300
years between Magistrate Edward Rowe, my direct ancestor, and
me. But the sallow complexion, the dark brown, black, or green
eyes (my father's were green), and the curved, black eyebrows
appear to have great carrying power.

Edward Rowe married his second wife, Mary, around 1861 and
on November 26, 1864 another son was born, Eli, my father.
Here we face a little mystery. Why did Edward Rowe give his off-
spring just one name, and such a short one at that? The name Eli
had been used for one of my grandfather's brothers, but that did
not answer the riddle; nor could my father offer an answer.

---

* Dunc died some two years ago. His younger brother, Gus, also became a prominent
  doctor, famous for, among other things, his work in the field of geriatrics.

My father was inclined to be physically delicate, and at first his parents were doubtful that he would survive. Perhaps it was this fact that made Edward so solicitous, encouraging his son in his schoolwork and promising that when Eli was finished at the local school he would be sent to St. John's to further his studies. Not that the young boy needed any pushing. As he grew stronger physically, he clung devotedly to the chances provided by his teacher, Phillip Newell. The school at Seldom was one of the "society" schools* and Newell was a first-class teacher, relatively speaking.

But fate had other things in store. When Eli was around 11 years old, his father Edward developed a painful swelling in one arm, probably due to one of the diseases associated with the cod or seal fisheries. Edward, one of the strongest men in northeastern Newfoundland, was inclined to be somewhat nonchalant about the matter; but his family urged him to walk across the island to the community of Fogo, where a medical doctor was established, and eventually he accepted their advice. When the doctor saw the swelling he followed the hallowed tradition: picking one of his instruments, he made several incisions in the swollen arm. My grandfather died agonizingly three days later, most probably a victim of septicemia brought about by the unsanitary lance. So the plans for his scholastic young son came to naught, since it was unlikely that her sons by the previous marriage to Captain Henry Osborne would assume any obligation in the matter, and Mary Rowe had no income and several dependent children. (Her sons by Captain Osborne were now adults with responsibilities of their own.)

Now that Mary was a widow, her friends in Seldom told her about the existence of a government program, usually called the "widow's mite," whereby rations of Indian meal and molasses were available from a "relieving officer" in the town of Fogo. My grandmother resisted the idea strongly, since then, as now, a goodly portion of Newfoundlanders object to what they regard as a species of government dole. Finally, in the interests of her children, she walked the ten miles to Fogo, applied for and obtained her order, and walked the ten miles back to Seldom. But after eating some of the food her children became seriously ill. One

---

* In the 18th and 19th centuries several societies were formed, usually under the auspices of the churches, to relieve the appalling literacy rates in the colony. Newell taught in the Seldom school.

experience was enough; when the children had recovered, Mary took a solemn oath that never again would she touch any kind of government charity, a promise she kept until her death in Burnt Bay (Lewisporte) some years later.

In the interim, with Eli old enough to assist in the fishery, and with her own work and no doubt assistance from her Osborne sons, Mary Rowe carried on. When her sons decided they should all take up residence in Burnt Bay, Eli went with her. He remained with the Osborne family until he married one of the Burnt Bay girls, Phoebe Ann Freake, and in time was able to set up their own home.

The other Rowe men, my grandfather's sons by his first wife, did not leave Fogo Island, preferring to carry on their lucrative fishery from Seldom. They were primarily "inshore" fishermen; whereas the Osborne men, in which I now include my father, "shipped for the Labrador" — which meant sailing to the Labrador in the spring as soon as ice conditions permitted, fishing on its coast in the summer, and returning to Newfoundland in the fall.* Thus, early in the 1880s, Eli Rowe, the only surviving son of Edward Rowe by his second wife, was living in Burnt Bay with his mother, Mary Rowe, and his half-brother James Osborne. There a new life awaited him.

---

* In both the inshore and the Labrador fisheries, the fish had to be salted and sun-cured and then taken to St. John's to be sold to the fish merchants there.

5 *The Structures of Higher Education*

*T*eaching was one job that a young person could be pretty sure of getting if he or she completed the high school grades. By 1928 the system had pretty well solidified, and in all, there were five grades of teacher. These were: *Grade 3*, which required Grade 11 plus one summer school, *Grade 2*, which required Grade 11 with two summer schools, and *Grade 1*, which required Grade 11 matriculation plus a semester of training at the Normal School. There were then two other, more advanced grades: *Associate*, which required a Grade 1 plus one successful year at university, and *University*, which required Grade 1 plus two successful years at university.

Two terms used above whose meanings were taken for granted in 1928 may need some elaboration and explanation today for the general reader. "Matriculation," for example, meant the standard that must be attained in order for a student to qualify for entrance to university; in Newfoundland's case matriculation meant taking a group of preparatory courses without which entrance to university was impossible. These courses were usually English, mathematics, a foreign language (usually French or Latin), a science (usually physics or chemistry, but sometimes botany or physiography could be substituted), and one or two other courses of which one was usually history.

"Normal school" meant (and still means) a teacher training institution. The first semester lasted from early September to late December and the second, with a new group of students, from early January to late June. In general, the September group had to meet higher standards than did the one in January, although there were some exceptions. The emphasis for both groups was almost entirely on academic work. There was, however, a slight concession made to the physical side of education once or twice a week, when a World War I veteran led the male students in arm and leg movements and stressed the value of hygiene. A female staff member did the same for the women.

When I started, the Normal School, unlike other institutions such as the denominational colleges and Memorial University College, had no organized games or sports. When I became aware of this appalling fact and of the equally appalling fact that the anti-sports members of the staff seemed to dominate the curriculum, I decided to go to the principal, Dr. Solomon Whiteway, and confront him with the discriminatory aspects of Normal School education. Dr. Whiteway was easily convinced that something could and should be done, and even when I made the argument for the foundation of a football (soccer) team, which of necessity would impinge on time allocated for academic work, he gave me his blessing.

As a result, the timetables for those who wished to play football had to be changed. This fact, to put it mildly, annoyed some of the staff; but when Helen Lodge, the vice-principal, challenged me for disrupting things, all I did was smile while reminding her that the arrangement had been approved by the principal. Needless to say, the women students and those few men who did not play football followed our progress avidly, especially when it became clear that the Normal School could hold its own against any of the other institutional teams. This success was well-nigh incomprehensible to the St. John's groups, who customarily regarded the Normal School students, especially those who came from the outports, as a bunch of incompetents.

In fact, when I entered Normal School in 1930, I was informed that the standards even then had improved considerably over those of previous years. Whatever the reason, the Normal School was beginning to overcome some of its inferiority complex, and not only in sports.

It was well known, for example, that Memorial had a Literary Society for lectures, debates, etc. So I and several kindred spirits, including in particular one Gladys Baird, who had a B.A. and wished to teach school, formed a similar society for the Normal School, and soon issued a challenge to Memorial to debate. On that day, the auditorium of Memorial was crowded as Gladys and I, representing the Normal School, defeated the best that Memorial could produce.

With the onslaught of the Great Depression, the government decided that one part of its program of economies would be to close the Normal School entirely. This, of course, aroused much criticism, since it meant that Newfoundland was left with no teacher training facilities of any kind. But instead of restoring the Normal School as it had been known for more than a decade — i.e. as an independent body operating under the aegis of the Department of Education — important innovations were instituted. It was decided to set up a teacher training department under the university, and, as well, to make the training session a full year long.

Even with these changes, however, there was still a tendency to regard the Normal School group as interlopers, in spite of the fact that Education was now the largest faculty. For example, before 1935 most of the important student posts at Memorial were filled by city students. But gradually changes emerged: in 1934-1935 the president of the Students' Representative Council (SRC) at Memorial was an outport student, Fred Gover of Bell Island; in 1935-1936 I was the elected secretary of the Literary Society, probably the most active and best known of the student societies; in June of 1936 I was elected valedictorian for the graduating convocation ceremonies; and in 1936-1937, another outport student, George Clarke, in a university general election, was chosen president of the SRC. Clearly, the stranglehold that St. John's had held for a decade was broken.

Later it became more and more evident that students were

beginning to think of themselves as Newfoundland and Canadian students rather than "town and gown." With its creation as a full-fledged, degree-granting university in 1949, Memorial started to grow, slowly for several years but in giant leaps from 1955 on. With thousands of students coming in to Memorial from communities of every size in Newfoundland, Memorial simply became too mixed to be fragmented either numerically or psychologically. It was now a Newfoundland and a Canadian institution.

Mention was made earlier in this chapter of the summer school. Since I lectured at these schools for eight summers, I learned of their value both academically and socially. The majority of these students came from small- or medium-sized communities, and until attending summer school had lived isolated and deprived lives. Yet I never ceased to marvel at how in the space of just one month these young students, most of them at the Grade 11 level, were able to improve their deportment and appearance. Equally astonishing was the speed with which, as summer wore on, they acquired both culture and sophistication. The summer school opened the doors of a new world to them and few failed to enter those doors.

In general, the history of the denominational colleges has been told, but certain aspects still need elaboration. One aspect usually ignored is that, originally, when the government decided to set up the colleges, both the Roman Catholics and the Anglicans tried to make them denominational. It was the success of the Roman Catholic Church in this matter that encouraged influential members of the Church of England, representing one-third of the total population, to fight for and receive similar rights. This, in turn, led inevitably to a demand from the Methodist or Wesleyan group, soon to reach 25 percent of the total population, that if the two larger churches could claim special treatment, the third largest could do likewise. The result of these conflicting claims was that the Catholic Church was recognized for higher or college education in 1843, and some eight years later the other two large denominations received similar treatment.* The new setup meant that the Catholic and Anglican churches each created two colleges, one for boys and one for girls. The Methodist church, as well, practised a degree of sexual segregation.

---

* In fact, the Anglican Church under Bishop Edward Feild had ignored the government Protestant college and had followed on the heels of the Catholic Church without government sanction.

The new colleges were unique in Newfoundland in a number of ways:

- They received large government grants.
- They had the right to charge relatively large fees.
- In general, the principal and staff for these institutions were brought to Newfoundland from the British Isles.
- The educational programs were far richer than those in ordinary Newfoundland schools. Only Harbour Grace and Carbonear, the two largest schools outside St. John's, were able to compete successfully, and this only as a result of community effort going back almost to the beginning of the century.
- Emphasis was placed on physical education, and especially on soccer, rugby, and cricket. The girls competed in field hockey.
- Each college had science facilities, a library, and indoor gymnasium facilities.
- In theory, every college was available to children of all classes, but in practice a majority of children could not afford the costs involved. Moreover, also in theory, pupils could leave their primary and elementary schools at specified stages, but in practice psychological barriers entered the picture.

It should be mentioned that there were many Anglicans who, to begin with, were against denominational colleges on principle, and even felt that, for practical reasons, the Anglicans and Methodists should act as one. This almost certainly would have encouraged the Presbyterians or Congregationalists, as well as any other smaller Protestant groups, to join the two larger groups.

PART

_2_

*THE
TEACHING
YEARS
1929–1948*

chapter

6 *The Teacher Emerges*

*I*n the autumn of 1929, while I was still trying to scrape together enough money to go to college for a year or two, Mr. Reynolds, our Lewisporte clergyman and chairman of the school board in and around Lewisporte, visited our house with an offer for me. It seemed that Little Burnt Bay, which at that time had only a half-year school running from September to February, had been sent a young teacher who, when he saw the nature of the village — there were 11 or 12 miles of wilderness from Lewisporte to the school — simply went back home. What Mr. Reynolds had to offer me was a teaching post at this school for the coming five months at $25 a month. (At that time, I had no teacher's certificate and therefore could not claim the augmentation to which graded teachers were entitled.) I was to have four pupils, one of whom was, I believe, in Grade 4.

I was inclined to accept, but before deciding I checked with my parents and to my no great surprise they both advised against it.

In fact, my father, recognizing that I was trying to collect some money, offered to give me $25 a month in return for performing some duties that he felt I could discharge in the store. But as I cogitated about the matter I realized that more than money was involved. I was 16 and had never been away from my father for more than a few days. I knew that I had led something of a sheltered life and that I had to make the break sooner or later. So I accepted the offer despite my parents' advice.

When she found out about my decision, my mother was filled with foreboding. Both of my parents were aware of the primitive conditions under which many Newfoundland people lived at that time. In addition to the physical deprivation which was so common, such factors as loneliness often became a serious consideration.

Nevertheless, I did stay the whole four months. When my father had learned my decision, he had taken me aside to give me this piece of advice: "My son, no doubt your buddies are all predicting that you won't be there very long. You don't have to go, but if you do I hope you will stick it out, and not give them the satisfaction of having you as a butt of their jokes." On a number of occasions during the fall when I was sorely tempted to give up, I recalled my father's advice. In addition, two activities sustained me. One was the convenience of being able to cut wood only a few yards from the house (though not many yards from a black bear), and the other was the fact that on those weekends when I travelled the 12 miles to my home (by running, or, when I was lucky, by motorboat), I was able to pick up from my parents enough reading matter to keep me sane until next time.

After my stint at Little Burnt Bay, I was lucky enough to be able to register at Prince of Wales College in the New Year, where I obtained my Grade 11 matriculation in June. This qualified me to attend Normal School in September. I graduated from Normal at Christmas as a qualified Grade 1 teacher.

Actually, I had had grandiose visions of becoming a lawyer, and to explain why I did not, it is necessary to describe the circumstances confronting young people at that time.

Elsewhere I have pointed out how difficult it was to get work even when one had a reasonable amount of basic education, i.e. Grade 11 matriculation or better. The few jobs offered in 1930 were meagre and, for the most part, unattractive. For boys there were logging and fishing for the physically inclined, and teaching and clerical work for the more intellectual. The alternative was to pack up and try to get to Toronto or some other city.

The teaching posts available were the result of Sir Richard Squires's emphasis on education in the late 1920s and even in the early 1930s.* But one fact that lessened the attractiveness of these jobs was that, once in a teaching job, a person found it virtually impossible to get out of it, as other academic or professional jobs required an uninterrupted course of study. To return to my own case, becoming a lawyer required that I stay in college or university straight through until graduation. But that was impossible without a steady supply of money. An outport student needed about $600 a year to go to St. John's. That kind of money was simply not available, and, of course, total cost was much more than that of one year. From matriculation to graduation took generally five years, of which three had to be spent at a mainland university. Few students could come up with that much money without breaking the sequence, a hiatus that most university authorities frowned on.

Of course, some students, especially those who came from the larger outports, were lucky enough to have well-to-do relatives who could lend money on occasion. While they were exceptions, it happened often enough to be meaningful to quite a few high school students around Newfoundland.

To illustrate, let me jump ahead to an incident that occurred when I was a school principal. Alex was a promising student who, according to the Otis I.Q. tests, was the brightest in his class. His father and mother, both admirable citizens, hoped to be able to save up enough to put him part-way through university a kind of task which, because of World War II inflation, was becoming more formidable every day. One day Alex's father and I got into a chat which led up to this request for advice: "Alex wants to go to Memorial and Dal [Dalhousie] to become a lawyer but I can't see any likelihood of that. We simply don't have the money to see him through to the end." Now, I knew that several of Alex's relatives, who had no children of their own, or few, also had several hundred thousand dollars at their disposal; my reaction, therefore, was as follows: "Jim," I said, "If I had to keep my boys out of university because I lacked money while my uncle rolled in wealth, I would be ashamed to admit I belonged to this place. My advice is,

---

* Sir Richard Squires, who was the prime minister of Newfoundland at the time, showed a keen interest in education.

send Alex to university and when he has run out of money go to Uncle Frank and ask to borrow the rest." And in the end this is what happened; the boy went on to law school, did exceptionally well, and is now the Honourable T. Alex Hickman, Chief Justice of Newfoundland. I do not take credit for this, and in fact I'm quite sure that without my advice much the same result would have occurred; but at least I encouraged him and his parents, and I was on the winning side.

After allowing for these exceptions, we are left with the fact that in Newfoundland before 1950, the large majority of students, even after meeting matriculation requirements, were unable to continue with their studies, a situation aggravated by the reality of large families. As far as girls were concerned, the situation was still less bright. Some girls did reach Grade 11, but the number was abysmally small. The thinking was that a girl's place was in the house, and if she spent much time outside it was only to do domestic work which ordinarily would have been done by the boys and men.

At the end of the term, Normal School graduates made arrangements to meet with the appropriate superintendents privately, for the custom was that the Superintendent of Education assisted boards of education in getting satisfactory teachers.

I had heard about Dr. L. R. Curtis, who had been the United Church's "pope" for nearly 40 years; one approached him with a suitable appearance of fear and trembling, and with good reason. Nevertheless, I hoped that I could get a school in some fairly sophisticated place similar to my own home town. Immediately upon satisfying himself that I did want a teaching post, Dr. Curtis informed me that there was an excellent school for me at a place called Wild Cove.* I had no idea where Wild Cove was and I tried to temporize. In the chitchat that followed he made reference to the fact that I would enjoy the church services. I nodded my agreement to this, but was soon astounded to learn that I would be enjoying my own services since there was no clergyman there.

Our meeting now took a more serious turn. When I told him I could not hold church services he challenged me at once. "Why

---

* Twenty-five years later I became the member of the House of Assembly in Newfoundland for White Bay South, a district that included Wild Cove, and in two provincial elections the voters gave me 100 percent of the vote.

not?" he asked. I told him that I did not think I was worthy of such an honour and responsibility. He again challenged me head-on: "Are you converted?" Again I temporized, saying that I wasn't too sure what conversion meant. I did not fool him there, how-ever: how anyone brought up in Lewisporte could fail to know what conversion meant was beyond comprehension. He lined me up for the final onslaught: "Have you made a public profession of your love for Jesus Christ?" "No, sir." "Then you are not con-verted." A pause. "I'm afraid there is nothing more I can do for you," he said. "Good day, sir." And there I was, two days before Christmas, without money and without a job.

I went home to Lewisporte the next day and gave my parents the (to them) good news—they would need me in the store and around the house. But three days later the telegraph messenger arrived at our house with a telegram for me: "Take next train for Bonne Bay." It was signed "L. Curtis."

Perhaps I should have mentioned earlier that while I was wait-ing in Dr. Curtis's office I chatted with his secretary, a very pleas-ant young lady who advised me privately to keep my chin up. Whether she had anything to do with the telegram and my appointment I do not know.*

My decision to accept Dr. Curtis's offer was motivated in part by the effect of an appealing, full-page picture of Bonne Bay in the old *Newfoundland Geography*. The picture showed a very level stretch of land (something not too common in Newfound-land) surrounded by mountains, with a number of fairly large, attractive homes.

I had no idea how to get to Bonne Bay, but some of our railway and nautical people were able to direct me. I had to buy a rail ticket to Humbermouth or Curling (now part of the city of Corner Brook). A few hours after the train reached Bay of Islands, the steamer (in my case the *Sagona*) set off for Bonne Bay, arriving there after dark on December 30. I did not know it at the time I left Lewisporte, but there was a separate, shorter way to reach Woody Point (the "capital" of Bonne Bay). This was a land route from Deer Lake to Lomond, 30-odd miles, or from Deer Lake on to Woody Point by going around the western arm of Bonne Bay on foot or by horse or dog team. But if the weather was fine the

---

* Many years later she became my secretary when I was Minister of Education and we never stopped being good friends from then until her retirement and death a few years ago. Kay Baird was a jewel!

Bay of Islands route, which was not much longer, was certainly more agreeable.

I knew little of Bonne Bay that first night. In fact I had to be told that my final destination and future home, while indeed part of Bonne Bay, was really Curzon Village, separated from Woody Point by geography and religion. Bonne Bay actually comprised eight or nine communities, none with more than 300 or 400 residents: Woody Point, Curzon Village (these two had close connections), Winter House Brook, St. Joseph's Cove, Shoal Brook, Birchy Head, Glenburnie, Norris Point, and Rocky Harbour. The soil was excellent, and fish of one kind or another — often cod and herring — were usually available; but the one compelling attraction was the mountains on the arms of fjords that enclose the bay, of which the two best known were the Table Land and Gros Morne. Both were sometimes indescribably beautiful; the former has the distinction of being the only mountain in Newfoundland to carry snow all year round; the latter looks much like a tortoise and at times during the winter becomes a mound of gold. Not surprisingly, the entire area of Bonne Bay is now a national park — Gros Morne National Park, to give it its official title.

The geographic division between Curzon Village and Woody Point was really only the road; the religious division lay in the fact that most of Curzon Village was United Church while practically all of Woody Point was Church of England. There were other distinctions between the two places due to the fact that Woody Point was the commercial centre of Bonne Bay, with large wharves capable of dealing with the largest ships likely to call there, and shops and other facilities; and the fact that government officials such as the magistrate, the doctor, and the customs officers were nearly all stationed at Woody Point.

With the two communities so near to each other, it was inevitable that there would be close social relations, and there was much intermarriage between the two groups. However, it was still true that the residents of Curzon, being United Church, were inclined to be more restrictive than the residents of Woody Point, most of whom were Anglican. Some of the old Curzon Village residents frowned on such frivolity as "social games," which term was really only a euphemism for the wickedness of dancing, smoking, cardplaying, and use of alcohol. I had been warned about this intolerance; in fact, I was not long in running into a minor piece of it.

On the first day that I walked from Curzon Village to Woody Point I happened to be smoking a cigarette. A venerable gentleman dressed in black came down the hill, and we stopped to greet each other. The conversation went much as follows:

*Uncle Billy:** I sees you smokes.

I.: Oh, excuse me, I forgot. Will you have a cigarette?

Uncle Billy: No. If 'twas Jesus Christ instead of me here this morning, would you offer him a cigarette?

I.: Yes, I would. 'Twould be up to himself whether he would accept one.

Uncle Billy: I think you'd have a job to get him to smoke one.

A few other encounters of this kind were about all that I experienced. When I began steadily dating Edie, the girl who became my fiancée (about whom more in the next chapter), which involved attending dances, plays, and concerts, there was some grumbling. But none of it was very serious and, after all, I had been born and brought up in one of Newfoundland's Methodist centres, where most of us were well trained in the art of dealing with what amounted to intolerance.

The double settlement of Woody Point and Curzon Village, while only small, carried far more importance than its size would indicate—partly because of the concentration of government officials there, but even more, perhaps, because of the fact that a number of the leading businessmen on the west coast were centred there. There was, therefore, even after the Depression struck in 1931, a disproportionately large social life. For example, it was never difficult to form a bridge foursome, something hardly likely to be true in most Newfoundland outports. As indicated above, the Anglican Church was quite free in its attitude to social activities, and scarcely a week went by without a public dance. To this would be added the functions such as dinners and "socials," which would be held on the church or school premises. There were two school buildings, the Anglican being a two-room and the United Church (mine) a one-room; and three church buildings, one Anglican, one United Church, and one Roman Catholic, which were less than a half-mile apart. (The small minority of a dozen or so Catholic families were scattered from Woody Point to Winter House Brook.)

---

* He was a complete stranger to me, a fact which was not very important to any Newfoundlander. I recall his telling me that his name was Billy, and in Newfoundland to greet an elderly man as "Uncle" was and is a mark of respect and friendliness.

My school in Curzon Village was, to use the popular vernacular, "one-room" or "sole-charge," which meant that the school might handle the whole range from kindergarten to Grade 11; in fact, for the two-and-a-half years I was there that was the situation. This work load created a problem. Because of its impressive record,* a number of the Anglican families would sometimes have their children register into the United Church school, which became embarrassing when the sole-charge teacher found himself or herself having to care for more children than did the two Anglican teachers together. Eventually the United Church board felt it had no choice but to send the Anglican children back to their own school, a decision that aroused considerable resentment among the children and parents involved. This was one of the first occasions on which I encountered the phenomenon of two or more church groups being quite happy, apparently, to integrate their educational services.

My years at Curzon Village were, for the most part, happy ones. I had an excellent boarding place with the Taylors, who were descended from the Carbonear families with that name. Captain Herb Taylor had built this first-class house around the end of World War I, a prosperous time. Since there were steep slopes and mountains only a few hundred feet to the back of the house, it had been quite easy to get a water supply by gravity. The house was large and extremely well built; all it lacked was electricity, but since I had lived most of my life without electricity, this was no great hardship.

The Taylor house also had one advantage not available to very many Bonne Bay people. It was the house in Curzon Village with a telephone service connected to every community in Bonne Bay. Each village had at least one house like this that connected to the other villages. In turn, each village was connected with the main post and telegraph office at Woody Point, from which there was contact with the outside world via Deer Lake. As a result of this system, there was far less isolation than one might expect. A message from Woody Point could sometimes be in the hands of a recipient in, say, St. John's in a matter of minutes, and, by the same token, a sender in Carbonear could usually have a message

---

* For the 15 years preceding my appointment the school had been staffed by a well-trained woman whose record as shown by the external public examinations was one of the best in Newfoundland.

delivered in Woody Point in less than an hour. Where the message's destination was Curzon Village, it would be relayed to the appropriate home in a few minutes, and if it was Trout River, ten miles away, the matter could be handled in a few minutes by the secondary telephone system.

The real isolation for any Bonne Bay community lay in the road and water systems, or rather the lack of such. A resident of Woody Point wanting to go inland to Deer Lake in the wintertime had to spend the better part of two days covering the 42 miles. Since there was no road other than a cow path, this meant there was nothing faster than the winter horse or dog team, which gave priority to the mail, and was only able to accommodate the occasional passenger when driving was smooth. It was not until the late 1940s that a permanent gravel road was completed from Deer Lake to Bonne Bay!*

By 1933 I had been in Bonne Bay two-and-a-half years, trying under most difficult circumstances to handle all the grades and doing everything possible to enable my bright pupils to complete their high school and go on to higher things. I still recall with gratitude the cooperation I received from both pupils and teachers, but it was an uphill job all the time. By the spring of 1933 it was clear to me that staying on in a one-room school, attractive as it was in some ways, could lead only to frustration. In fact, from the standpoint of my own studies I had already fallen behind by several academic courses which I could have taken extramurally had I not been so preoccupied with social activities, a girl friend, and of course a heavy school load.

There was also the financial side of my situation. As a teacher with Grade 1 status, I had started my Bonne Bay teaching at $70 a month. My boarding cost only $20 a month and was excellent; with indoor plumbing, and proprietors who were more than generous, I could not have asked for better conditions. But as a result of the Depression, in September of that year my salary was cut and by 1932 it was cut again. The $70 that would have enabled me to live in comfort, and within two years to go back to university, was cut to a total of $28 a month, which was not even enough to supply me with the basics of life. My only recourse was

---

* That road is now entirely paved and, while somewhat twisty at times because of the mountains, it is considered one of the best secondary highways in the province. This and Bonne Bay's other assets — the bay itself, the towering poplars, the large and beautiful homes — combine to make Bonne Bay one of the most beautiful spots in all Newfoundland.

to my parents, who by now were receiving requests from other members of the family.

Since I would not contemplate dependence on my parents, I decided to leave Bonne Bay to engage in extramural studies, and possibly find a better-paying school.

And so it was good-bye to what was, and is, surely one of the most beautiful parts of Canada. The great fjords, the streams cascading off the mountain, the topless poplars, the almost palatial homes, the luxuriant vegetation, and above all the lovely girls, the countless friends, the golden tableland, the mighty Gros Morne which somehow always seemed to be shining, and my girl-friend—all had to left behind.

7 *Bishops Falls, Lewisporte, and Memorial*

*L*eaving Bonne Bay permanently was a wrench for me. I had a lot of friends there, and my love affair with a Bonne Bay girl had not diminished during the two-and-a-half years.

Edith Butt was the youngest daughter of George C. Butt, for many years the leading merchant on the west coast of Newfoundland. The Butts were one of the old families of Newfoundland, having settled in Crocker's Cove and Carbonear in the 1700s. In some period one or more families moved north to a thriving fishing commuity in Notre Dame Bay called Exploits. Eventually some of the Exploits Butts moved to Quebec; later, they came back to Newfoundland by way of Bay St. George, where in time they became one of the largest and best-known families of that bay.

From Sandy Point in Bay St. George, one James Butt moved

north along the coast to reach Chimney Cove and then Trout River, where he founded a thriving business in the herring and cod fishery; from there he moved to Woody Point. His sons George and Walter rapidly developed the fishery into the best-known firm on the coast, reaching as far north as Battle Harbour on the Labrador side of the Strait of Belle Isle.

One of these brothers, George, was Edie's father and, of course, became the grandfather of our son Bill (who is now a St. John's lawyer). In the meantime, an Elizabeth Butt of Exploits had married Josiah Manuel, a leading Notre Dame Bay merchant. Their daughter Mitchie married John Crosbie (grandfather to John Crosbie of the Conservatives), and the Crosbies' daughter Olga became the mother of Penny, who married our Bill. Thus Penny and Bill were distantly related, though neither knew it at the time.*

Although my wife-to-be was a member of one of Newfoundland's wealthier families, marriage was out of the question on $30 a month. In any event, 20 or 21 years was hardly a mature enough age to get married. My father, whose business was still fairly vigorous, argued that living at home doing extramural university studies (since I couldn't afford full-time residential studies) was probably the most profitable way to spend a year. So when I resigned from my Curzon Village school in June of 1933, I made no attempt to obtain a job for that fall.

The university program enabled students to obtain credits while staying at home — or better still while working at short-term jobs, etc. Competent students could take two correspondence courses in a year. Accordingly, in September of 1933 I started studying English and history at home.

Life in Lewisporte was very pleasant. Though there were fewer than 600 inhabitants, it still provided superior social amenities and opportunity. For example, I was the captain of the Lewisporte soccer team and participated in just about every activity to be found in that sphere: bridge, church choir, debates, and socials (i.e. mild forms of dancing). But in spite of this, as the fall wore on I found myself beginning to worry over my self-imposed

---

* Though this is a digression, I feel it is worth telling, since it illustrates a situation that is probably quite common in Newfoundland. It was, however, and still is a cardinal fact of human relations in Newfoundland that *close* relatives do not marry each other. It is generally recognized in Newfoundland that, apart from any religious or legal restrictions, it might be potentially dangerous genetically for any close relatives, e.g. first cousins, to marry.

working restrictions as far as remunerative employment was concerned. Nor was it sufficient to tell myself that I was doing nearly a half-year of university work which in two or three years would translate into dollars and cents.

Then something happened that was almost a repeat of what had happened when I graduated from Normal School three years before. A teacher at Bishops Falls became ill and Dr. Curtis, who had been favourably impressed with my Bonne Bay record, invited me to take over the "Station" school in Bishops. After convincing myself that I would still be able to carry the two school courses, I accepted. And so, around three in the morning on the bitter night of January 2, 1934, I arrived at Bishops Falls. I had a married cousin with whom I could find temporary shelter, but instead I chose to walk the streets until daylight. It was cold, but not intolerable, and I had taken a precaution which on several occasions I had found indispensable and which I consistently followed: that of wearing plenty of warm clothing literally from head to toe.

Even then, Bishops Falls was one of the most prosperous towns in Newfoundland. Its strategic position on the river made it possible to generate electricity which was then supplied to several towns in the area, but more important was the fact that it made possible the building and operation of a large pulp mill which pumped its product upstream some ten miles to Grand Falls, where the pulp became paper. In addition to being a hydro and pulp-producing centre, Bishops was also a railway centre. The main line of the Newfoundland Railway, together with its several branches, took in nearly 1000 miles. While St. John's was the headquarters of the line, right from the first it was recognized that a second headquarters was necessary. This meant that a roundhouse, dispatchers, coal (later oil) facilities, and other items had to be duplicated at Bishops Falls. In short, Bishops was a busy centre with full employment, and since it had unlimited supplies of electricity the standard of living was far superior to that of most towns its size. Its shops were large and well stocked.

Bishops was also a nodal point for logging operations. Thus, in the fall or winter hundreds of loggers would first converge on Bishops from scores of places within a radius of 100 miles or so. From Bishops they radiated to the various logging areas, where they lived in logging camps for the three or four months during which they cut the spruce and fir to be converted into paper. When the cut was over, the loggers once more converged on

Bishops, from where they would set off for their home communities, most of which were in Notre Dame Bay. At both stopovers, during the hours or days they waited for transportation (usually in trains)—sometimes wearing nothing more than their logans or skin-boots,* and the heavy work clothes they had worn all winter —men needed clothes, a demand that the Bishops merchants were only too glad to satisfy.

In one sense it was a pity that Bishops Falls was overshadowed by its much larger and much more sophisticated neighbour, Grand Falls, but the former still had many attractions in addition to its prosperity. In some respects the social life resembled that of Bonne Bay, with the qualification that Bishops was larger and in some respects was more cultured. The town was sportsminded, with Newfoundland's largest river for skating and swimming; every Saturday night the Catholics held a dance that was patronized by other denominations; and there were other frequent social events such as plays, concerts, and card games. Bridge was always popular; for my part, I helped to form a bridge club that operated for some four months.

I did not stay long at Bishops, but perhaps an overview of the school system would be valuable. Educationally, Bishops was divided in three. At the eastern end, where the pulp mill operated, were three or four teachers, which allowed classes to be separated by grades; at the middle of town, where most of the Catholics lived, was a two-classroom school; and at the west end—the "station"—was the one-classroom school in which I taught.† My grades ran from kindergarten to Grade 8; at peak times I had over 70 students. The majority were the children of train workers, and for the most part well looked after—a reflection of the good earnings of their fathers.

It would have been quite pleasant to continue to teach at Bishops but circumstances altered the case. That spring the United Church Board of Education invited me to become principal of the school I had attended through Grade 10 at Lewisporte. I was to begin in the fall, and the attractions were irresistible. Not

---

* *Skin-boots*, made from the skin of seals and other animals, were once very common in Newfoundland but are little used today. In their place are *logans*, a heavy, near-waterproof kind of footwear made mostly of plastic and rubber.

   Once the men reached home, of course, they did what their counterparts in New Brunswick, Quebec, etc. did: they "cleaned up."

† The west end of Bishops Falls contained the second most important headquarters of the Railway; the most important, of course, was the one at St. John's.

only could I be at home with a mother whose chief desire seemed to be to supply food to her son, but many of my old friends were still there, and my salary would be considerably higher than it had been for several years — though, to be sure, it would still be quite low.

I began as Principal of the three-room school in September of 1934. I knew my duties would be demanding; nevertheless, I had signed up with Memorial for another two courses designed to bring the university even nearer. (I had passed my previous two courses with better-than-average marks, an achievement not to be wondered at, since English and history were not much more difficult for me than "Little Red Riding Hood." In science and mathematics I had to work my head off, but literary courses were as easy as any fairy tale.) Thus after my Lewisporte year I would have completed four full university courses, leaving only six to complete in my second year for graduation from Memorial, an achievement which together with my Normal School training would give me all the teacher grades listed: 3rd, 2nd, 1st, Associate, and University. With University status the sky was the limit. It is true that there were other academic opportunities in the offing, but this did not invalidate the most important of the lot. There lay both prestige and money.

My year in Lewisporte as Principal was a pleasure beyond belief. No community of its size could excel Lewisporte for activity of every kind; not a week went by without something going on. We built a clubhouse so that dances and other social activities could be held without antagonizing church authorities, the Orange Lodge, or any of the other somewhat puritanical groups, but the club was not confined entirely to frivolous programs. Serious regular meetings were held and programs designed. And, of course, none of it interfered with the work of the other religious and social groups; rather, our work enhanced theirs.

By the end of my principalship, I had passed my second two courses and I felt certain I could handle the final six courses I needed, and even win one of the few scholarships available. If the university authorities would allow me to take six courses in one year instead of the usual five, I would be on the pig's back. After some discussion, President A. G. Hatcher gave me his active support, and I was once more on my way.

I had to muster all my resources to help pay my expenses of about $600, a rather daunting sum at that time. The previous academic year at Lewisporte had not been as profitable as I had anticipated. The reason for this was not simply my low salary as a principal (although it totalled something under $50 a month). In spite of the fact that, ignoring the worsening depression, Mother refused to charge me more than $15 a month, I did have to pay this amount. And the truth is that by the time I went to Lewisporte my supply of clothes in particular and of miscellaneous items generally had much decreased; on my arrival, a good deal of my earnings had been used to replenish this supply. Thus, by September, when I was getting ready for university, my supply of clothing etc. was not too bad, but my financial condition was. However, I did have some assurance from my father that he and my brother would do their best to assist me; and there were two other bright spots.

First, in that summer of 1935 the Commission of Government decided to take up the census, something that had not been done for about 14 years. This work was utterly fascinating and had the additional merit of providing a few welcome dollars. The census-taking was done on a piecemeal basis throughout August. I went the rounds with my closest friend, Art Budgell of Lewisporte, and the value of my work was computed at $106. That was excellent in itself, but since it was to be paid only in October or November, it did nothing to change the condition of my pockets for the two months or so before I got paid.

A still more promising prospect lay in the indenture system which had been in force for some years. What this amounted to was that students who were in financial need could borrow money from the government with an undertaking to repay the money after they had begun or returned to teaching. This generosity was in my view one of the best programs of the government, since it had the merit of inducing thousands to enter the teaching profession.

The census and the indenture system were godsends to me, whose financial circumstances were so stringent, but they did no more than meet about half my needs. One way or another, I had to raise another $300 or so. I finally did so in the only way I could: by borrowing small amounts ($10 to $20) from several of my university friends and somewhat larger amounts from family friends in Lewisporte. That I could do this was an indication of the respect and sympathy which my family commanded.

My first semester was very enjoyable. Memorial had been a goal that at one period I thought I would never attain. Now, here were all the things I loved: history; English; public speaking; languages; athletics of every kind such as soccer, tennis, badminton, skating and hockey, and basketball; the sheer fun of books and people. . . . The list was almost endless, and yet I managed to participate in just about all of them. Nor did my marks suffer: my Christmas examination results were excellent, and to my great joy I came first in Dr. A. C. Hunter's famous course, English 200, by common agreement among Memorial students the hardest course in the syllabus.

My standing in the first semester gave me confidence for the second, and, rightly or wrongly, I felt I had a good chance to come first for that term among the literary students, and, as I have said, perhaps earn a scholarship.

But, as today, when scholarships were involved, it seemed almost certain that the numerical mark got precedence, and it was our feeling that literary students simply did not have the same opportunity to make maximum marks as, say, math or physics students had. We saw that while mathematics students quite often got 100 percent, rarely did one hear this of a literary student. (In fact, in all my experience, while I have managed to get A + on all but one of my courses at Mount Allison and on all my courses at Toronto, I have never actually been given 100 percent. Yet on one occasion, when I challenged one of my professors on that issue, he told me that there was really no difference between A + and 100 percent.) This may not be so important today now that there are so many scholarships available, but in 1935 the number was so few that a scholarship, no matter how small, could mean the difference between academic life and death.

By the middle of the academic year at Memorial one could pinpoint with near-certainty who the successful second-year students would be. In the academic groups it looked to be a tossup eventually between another student and me.*

In April 1936, when everything seemed to be going well for me, I received a telegram from Dr. Knapp, the resident doctor at Lewisporte: "Regret to advise you your father suffered a massive

---

* It was almost certain, also, that within another year or two the other student would be making a try for the Rhodes Scholarship, and I was sure that he would eventually win this prestigious annual award. He did both. What about Rowe? Very simple: too old. One of the adamant rules of the Rhodes Scholarship was that you had to be under 25 and unmarried at the time of the award. This was fine for the candidates who had been born in St. John's, since they were very likely to have become eligible by the time they were 21 or 22; but it was not so good for the scores of students like me who for financial reasons had had to break the continuity of their education.

stroke last night. Survival doubtful." The world collapsed under my feet. Most severe of all, of course, was the effect on the family, especially my mother, who loved her husband to the point of idolatry. Yet my father did not die from the stroke; after being semi-conscious for several weeks he partly recovered.

In the meantime my brother had to try to keep the business going, but it was clear that the creditors were out of patience. Finally he and I had to contact the creditors personally to try to arrange a compromise. After several weeks we were successful in this, but when my father was able to finish his dealings with his creditors he did not have a dollar for his use.

The family all rallied round, of course, but for me all my university plans had been shattered. For example, though I was offered the Mount Allison Scholarship, which took care of tuition expenses at that university in Sackville, New Brunswick for two years, I had to turn it down. This would have been most welcome ordinarily, but since tuition represented only about a third of my total annual expenses, there was no point in accepting the scholarship; after Memorial, I could do nothing more than return to the teaching field.

In order to carry on for the two months or so left in the school year, I had to try to get financial help from my friends and relatives. This meant that, with the assistance I had to give my parents, I was going to be kept in a state of semi-servitude for a year or more, a prospect just as unattractive to my girlfriend (now financée) as it was to me.

Despite the Depression, friends and relatives came to my aid for a total of around $300 and I stayed on for the remaining months, graduating with first-class honours. I was once more number one in Dr. Hunter's famous English course, and achieved high honours as well in Professor Allen Fraser's history, economics, and political science courses).

The extracurricular aspect of my year at Memorial had also been very fulfilling. Our football team was still undefeated for the season, and it was one of the sorrows of my year at Memorial that the week the team was being photographed, I was at Lewisporte awaiting, as I thought, the imminent demise of my father. On the literary side, I had been elected to the Literary Society, generally recognized as the most active and prestigious society on the campus. This was all the more gratifying because I had not been at Memorial for several years. And when the time came to select the three editors of the university magazine *Cap and Gown*, to my surprise I was elected one of them.

Committee activities of the Society included speeches on Spain, Abyssinia, and Italian cities such as Sienna and Florence, and speeches on Carlyle and Ruskin. We also arranged a number of speeches by prominent people. (One was by the senior Newfoundlander in the Commission of Government, the Honourable F. C. Alderdice; unfortunately his illness and eventual death intervened.) Debates, ever popular in Newfoundland circles, attracted much attention.

The elected president of the Literary Society was Michael Harrington, a St. John's student later to become famous in literary matters as a poet and writer, and perhaps still more as editor of the *Evening Telegram*. Mike and I did not know each other well at that time, but we got along quite efficiently as a team. With handling all the arrangements for the speeches, debates, and other various activities of the Society, as well as participating in sports of one kind or another, Harrington and I were probably two of the busiest students on campus.

On top of all this came another surprise, an honour of the first order. The elections for male valedictorian, which were open to the student body, were usually highly exciting, with a good deal of lobbying; but traditionally a St. John's student was likely to be chosen. To my surprise and, I daresay, that of many others, when the election was over the chairman announced that the winner was Frederick W. Rowe of Lewisporte, Newfoundland. (Earlier I had won the Public Speaking Prize, again by popular vote.)

Once the news had sunk in I began thinking about and planning for the auspicious event. I knew that the new Newfoundland governor from Britain, Sir Humphrey Thomas Walwyn, was also scheduled to speak. It was my great hope that he would let me know something of what he intended to say; I was most anxious to be able to make my remarks pertinent to his. This turned out not to be possible, so in the end I had to speak extemporaneously, and here is where my outport speaking experience bore fruit. On graduation day Governor Walwyn spoke about selfishness, and told us to "put our shoulders to the wheel." My reaction to this was that with over half our population jobless there was little to be selfish about. The gist of my own speech was: "I agree. But will you or somebody show us where the wheel is?" and so on. My presentation was well received, and all but one of the Board of

Regents and other dignitaries on the platform congratulated me on it.

Here is a portion of my speech as recorded by a stenographer on that day in June of 1936:

> His Excellency, in the course of his remarks, urged that our motives for receiving an education should not be selfish ones. . . . when we came here we had no delusions as to what our course would mean to us afterwards. . . . We knew before we came here that already there were hundreds of college graduates walking the streets of almost every country, in enforced idleness. Our presence here, then, indicated three facts: first, that the thirst for knowledge had not decreased; second, that we still had faith in our country; and third, that we believed Memorial could help us to help Newfoundland.
>
> It is true that we cannot avoid becoming discouraged and cynical at times; that we get tired of being told to put our shoulder to the wheel when, in reality, we can't find the wheel itself; that we are going out into a world of doubt, confusion, and misery that is not of our making; that sometimes we feel we are indeed the forgotten generation. But it is also true that we are still proud to belong to Newfoundland; that we still have something of that indomitable spirit that sent our forefathers across the Atlantic to face difficulties a hundred times greater than we face today; that we have not yet lost our enthusiasm, our willingness to work and if need be to sacrifice. . . . We leave here today determined that we will do our part in trying to alleviate and mitigate some of the poverty and injustice, some of the misery and ignorance in Newfoundland.

Thus, I experienced the culmination of my year at Memorial, well worth the financial difficulty.

Earlier, in May of that year, the large United School at Wesleyville (with five, later six teachers) had invited my to apply for the principalship, and this I had done. I started in September. My fiancée, meanwhile, working in her father's business, had for some time been loyally waiting, a bit frustrated and seeing no reason why we could not pool our resources and get married. Since my salary at Wesleyville was $90 a month, an amount which, when systematically supplemented with Edie's savings, would enable us to live both comfortably and respectably while meeting all our obligations, I came round to the same conclusion, and in the fall of 1936 we set the date for that Christmas.

8 *Marriage and Wesleyville*

Getting married at Christmas turned out to be not as easy as it first appeared. Edie wanted to get married at home, and Bonne Bay was 42 miles from the nearest part of the Railway, which was Deer Lake, while Wesleyville was nearly 50 miles from the nearest part of the Railway in that vicinity. Moreover, since we had to keep a wary eye on the pack ice moving down the Newfoundland coast, everything had to be speeded up.

Accordingly, as soon as the schools closed for the Christmas vacation I took the passenger boat at Wesleyville to go to Gambo, where I could take the train, assuming of course that the train was not blocked by untoward weather. I arrived at Gambo after a long but otherwise pleasant trip punctuated from time to time by the slob ice forming because of the calm cold weather. There I received the unpleasant news that the only train available for the next 24 hours was a "way" freight, which only went as far as Notre Dame Junction and was probably the slowest train on earth. But there was one advantage to this. Lewisporte, my home town, was about 50 miles from Gambo and not that far out of my way; if I could get there I would have perhaps ten or twelve hours to spend with my family.

Things seemed to be going well when the freight arrived at

Gambo earlier than expected, and I proceeded to the Junction, where the Lewisporte branch train normally connected. But there I was greeted with more bad news. As I had expected, I arrived at the Junction at nightfall. This meant I could not continue until the next day, and ordinarily I would have been looked after by the station agent and his wife; but a few days ago their little boy had contracted a contagious disease (I believe it was whooping cough) and the family had been quarantined. All they could do was offer me shelter in a bitterly cold office, in which the potbellied stove, which was capable of heating two or three offices, could not be lighted for fear of contaminating personnel. I had no choice but to accept.

I made the best of it. I took my now-habitual precaution of putting on extra underwear, socks, sweaters, and fur cap. There was no bench or couch in the office, but there were ledgers that could be piled up and used for a pillow while I stretched out on the floor. These things being attended to, I drifted off into the deepest sleep I had ever known.

But things now took an alarming turn. Sometime during the night, Railway headquarters in St. John's was informed of my presence, and since the temperature was now well below normal the agent was ordered to risk contamination and get a coal fire going for me. The agent was only too glad to follow the advice, but what he did not take into account was that I had on enough clothes to look after two or three men. He now proceeded to make up for lost time by developing a fire that could have kept a dozen or more warm.

When I was awakened at 8 a.m. (through the strenuous efforts of the agent and his assistant), I found that all my inside clothes were soaking wet and I had to peel them off and dry them before I could venture outdoors. In the meantime I was stranded at Notre Dame Junction, with no chance to go anywhere until midnight when the No. 1 Express would reach the Junction on the way to the west coast. Thus, besides being delayed I would be forced to forgo the Lewisporte visit and board the Express, which made a stop at Deer Lake, the junction of the Bonne Bay Road. I fumed and sputtered to the small group, but I was helpless, as were the agent and his staff.

Then came a small miracle. At around 9 a.m. the agent came out of his office to announce that the branch train would be leaving Lewisporte for the Junction to get some freight; and of course if there were passengers lying around waiting for transportation it was the railway's bounden duty to lend a hand. When I arrived at 12 noon the train triumphantly blew the whistle and all Lewisporte wondered what the explanation was. I should add that I never did see any freight; nor did I see any passengers except one Frederick Rowe, who found himself being welcomed like the prodigal son.

I was able to spend the afternoon with my parents (my father had recovered enough from his stroke to move around and even do odd jobs), and go to a party that night which my Lewisporte associates held for me. Everything was free, as far as I was concerned, but as the hospitality included some of my cousin Arch's famous home brew, I paid for it the next morning as the train lumbered along to the Deer Lake mecca.

I almost paid for it that night in Lewisporte, for as a result of the good cheer, when I got home I lay on the couch to be able to have a full hour's rest before the branch train left. Unfortunately, I fell asleep, and even the train's whistle did not awaken me. When I did wake up I had only about 15 minutes to get to the station. I ran most of the way, dragging heavy luggage along with me, and reached the train just in time to avoid being left in Lewisporte. Once more I was dripping wet, and completely exhausted.

I reached Deer Lake in the morning, having spent the time on the train sitting up since I could not afford the extravagance of a sleeper. Normally the mail contractor could take one or two passengers on his dog sled, but I remember that for some reason (probably excessive mail) I had to walk the 42-mile length to Woody Point by way of the western arm of Bonne Bay.* I would not have to travel alone, however; to my great satisfaction I discovered that an employee of the Butt firm, George Brown, was also on the way to Woody Point, and of course he also had no choice but to walk.

George was a big-framed, powerful man who did his best to disguise his feeling that I was likely to give out somewhere along the trail. One good side of the walk was that while there was some snow down, it was not in drifts. We walked at top speed, because we wanted to keep within hailing distance of the dog team and we were equally concerned about reaching some habitable place by

---

* Bonne Bay has three arms, the first of which is too small to be visible on the map in this book: (1) the eastern arm; (2) the main arm, often called the "eastern arm"; and (3) the western arm, on which Woody Point was located.

nightfall. In retrospect I know now that we weren't really walking; it was nearer to a good jog.

Somewhere along that 30-mile stretch George and I ran into a traveller going the other way to connect with the train at Deer Lake. He brought good news: he had come from Woody Point by water, and the boat that he had taken was waiting for us at Lomond, a community located where the road route touched the main arm of the bay about 12 miles from our destination. This meant we would not need to walk that distance or have to find a log cabin or logging camp for resting before we went on.

Though it was an open boat, it was as welcome as any ocean yacht would have been. What George and I forgot to consider, however, was that for the previous 30 miles we had walked non-stop at a speed few could have equalled, and that for the entire walk we had sweated "like an ox." We were crammed in a boat that already was touching some slob ice, and now the thermometer took a nosedive to mark the beginning of what was to be one of the coldest nights of the year; had the boat broken down, George and I would probably have frozen to death. But apart from this fear everything went well, and three hours after leaving Lomond we were at the Butts' home at Woody Point. This meant we could get married on Christmas Day, and get married we did.

The wedding, held in the Butts' home, was a large one. The rooms were spacious, but so many were invited that four or five sittings had to be offered — each, of course with appropriate toasts to the couple. Since I had had practically no sleep for four nights, this meant that I had to do something that was barely possible: remain upright and try to look intelligent and interested when I was really in a state of at best semi-consciousness.

The Christmas Day wedding was followed by two more crises. The first danger was that either we would not get to Deer Lake in time to connect with the eastbound Express, or, what was equally serious, the Express would be delayed by snow and ice. The second danger was announced by the telegraphs from north-eastern Newfoundland: there was a possibility that the arctic ice would be blocking the northeast coast within another day or so, in which case my bride and I would be stuck for an unpredictable amount of time in Gambo unless we hurried. In view of these dangers we had no choice but to pack up just about everything we had (including my wife's huge trunk) and get going the day after Christmas.

Mr. Butt had engaged a large dog team for the luggage and a horse and sheltered (closed-in) sleigh where Edie would be completely comfortable. As for me, once more I had to walk 42 miles, this time with considerable snow to contend with. We left Edie's home around two in the afternoon and had covered about 14 miles (which included climbing the notorious "struggle"*) when we reached a logging camp, where the two drivers wisely insisted that we put up for the night.

We were up again before five the next morning and made ready for what we knew would be touch and go with the dogs, the horse, and the four human beings involved. Twice we stopped along the way to feed and rest the horses, but for the last ten miles or so it was most uncertain. We worried especially about the horse, because periodically it was swaying on its legs.

It was almost 12 o'clock when we reached the Deer Lake station, only to hear the beautiful news that because of conditions on the railway between Port aux Basques and Corner Brook the train would not reach Deer Lake until 2 a.m. If we had to have a delay, we would have preferred a longer one, as this gave us barely enough time to take advantage of the hospitality of Mr. and Mrs. George Wellon, close acquaintances of the Butts, who invited us to their home for a bath and some coffee; but sure enough, the Express pulled into Deer Lake at 2 a.m. We found ourselves the only passengers on the Pullman, and it may well have been the only time in the Railway's history when a Pullman went from Port aux Basques as far as Gambo with only two passengers, plus a porter who could attend to their needs full-time.

We arrived at Gambo some time after dark of that day and, true to his word, my friend Boyce Howse was there in his boat waiting for us, with Captain Sydney Hill, the famous sealer. We arrived at our destination, Wesleyville, around midnight. It had been a beautiful night, calm and cold, a forewarning of things to come; at dawn the next day there was heavy drift ice as far as we could see. Our luck had held to the end.

Wesleyville was one of the larger fishing communities in Newfoundland, with a population of around 1300. The majority of the working population were Labrador fishermen during the

---

* The "struggle" was a well-named stretch of the Bonne Bay Road lying between Glenburnie at the bottom of the western arm and the Lomond Road intersection. It was generally regarded as the steepest, highest, and most dangerous piece of road in Newfoundland.

summer, with some supplementary earnings from the seal hunt which normally took place during the months of March and April. A few of the male residents carried on some inshore fishing as well, but by far the mainstay of the economy was the Labrador operation.

This operation was conducted as follows. In May and June the crew, numbering from five or six to perhaps a dozen, fitted out their vessel, a schooner of anywhere from 30 or 40 tons to 100 tons or larger. As soon as the preparations, i.e. nets, traps, and jiggers, had been arranged, and if ice permitted, they took off for Labrador. The schooner went to a vacant and likely-looking spot on the Labrador coast, and was then securely anchored or tied to the shore while the crew put out their requisite gear. As a rule, they stayed on if fish were plentiful, but if fish turned out to be scarce in that spot, the vessel continued its northern cruising, sometimes going as far north as Saglek Bay or beyond. If they did not have to go searching for fish, the schooner was able to start its homeward journey in July. It was always possible that a storm or bad luck with fish or ice could ruin a summer's voyage; yet in spite of dangers and fishing failures, the Newfoundland fishermen continued their efforts, often against great odds, by sailing north as soon as conditions permitted.

At the time of my appointment to Wesleyville there were only 21 schooners sailing from that port, in contrast to the 50 or more of only a decade or so ago. Some effort was made to compensate for the shore fishery decline by trying to build up lobster, salmon, and other minor fisheries. As I have indicated, the seal fishery was probably the most important of the minor ones. The enterprise consisted in sending ships (usually steel-plated) in the spring to try to make contact with the ice floes, where young seals, only a few weeks old, would sometimes be available for the taking. Here, too, luck played a great part, as did the hazards; but the pelts were regarded as almost akin to gold dust.

From what I have said it is clear that Wesleyville differed completely from what I had experienced in Bonne Bay, Bishops Falls, and Lewisporte. Wesleyville was, in fact, the "compleat" fishing community. There was no road connection — contact with the rest of the world was mostly by water: passenger motorboats to Gambo, some 40 miles away, where connection could be made with the railway trains; and schooner or coastal steamer, which usually left once a week for St. John's, where the fish could be sold

Me at 7 months.

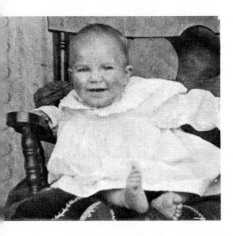

Me at age 14 in 1926.

Me at age 20.

Me in the early 1950s.

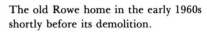
The old Rowe home in the early 1960s shortly before its demolition.

Clockwise from bottom right: Me, my sister Gladys (who died of diphtheria at the age of 10), my brother Harold, my sister Ethel, and my cousin Gordon Osborne.

A group of Lewisporte children and their teacher around 1921.

My parents.

The Butt home in winter.

Senior Lewisporte pupils, probably early World War I.

Bonne Bay in winter, probably in the 1920s or earlier.

The Curtis Academy opened in September 1943 and for a period it was the largest school in Newfoundland. I was its first principal.

One of the older sections of Bonne Bay, commonly called the "Anchorage." The Roman Catholic church is in the background. Probably 1920 or before.

The Rowe buses set off for the provincial elections. October 1971.

Gym class at Labrador City. Present were the Honourable Max and Mrs. Lane, Edie, and me.

Meeting Prime Minister Diefenbaker during his visit to Newfoundland for the opening of the new university, October 9, 1961.

Meeting Prime Minister St. Laurent under the Peace Tower in Ottawa, where he greeted delegates to the federal-provincial conference in 1957.

Smallwood and me at the University of Coimbra in
Portugal, where we were guests of President Salazar.

With Prime Minister Trudeau at the St. John's Arts and
Culture Centre during a summer visit in the early 1970s.

1954. Most boys in Lewisporte learned to swim before they reached their teens, and some at around age six. I was among the latter, and except for the period in the more isolated outports, I have continued swimming virtually on a daily basis ever since.

The four boys and their mother up a tree in Quincy, Massachusetts, 1948.

Family group. *Left to right:* Bill, Fred, Edie, me, Bud, and George.

to the merchants and supplies could be taken home for the winter.

There was a general shortage of some of the basic needs, like sanitation, road services, garbage collection, sewage services, and electricity and the many services provided by it. But nevertheless there was a great deal of prosperity, when one allows for the Depression, as evidenced by the excellence of a majority of the homes. Socially, Wesleyville exhibited all the virtues of the fishing community: loyalty to the church and other institutions, cooperation with the principal of the school and his staff, charity toward the less well-to-do, and a strong desire to maintain community standards.

I had been principal of the United Church school at Wesleyville since September. There were five United Church classrooms in the community, but before my second year there started, the central staff had to be enlarged from three to four, and with a feeder classroom at either end of the community, the school then had six rooms, all under my authority.

In the spring and summer before I had taken up residence in Wesleyville, I had discovered that the largest secondhand bookstore in Newfoundland, Garland's of St. John's, was going out of business and was selling thousands of books at ten cents a copy. In spite of my usual money shortage, I had got together enough to permit me to buy some of this bonanza. My recollection is that I bought about $20 worth, all of them hardcover and practically all classics published by such houses as Nelson, Dent, Collins, Houghton Mifflin, and Macmillan. But soon I was to derive even more benefit from this sale, and not just personally.

During that summer I was working in St. John's, packing books for the Department of Education. One day the chairman of the United Church Board of Education in Wesleyville, Rev. William Reid, looked me up. We got on very well, with the result that I felt free to make some suggestions to him. The school had no library of any kind, a deficiency that was reflected in many of the homes. I suggested to Mr. Reid that he authorize me to purchase several hundred Garland's books with a view to creating a school library. He agreed, and before I left St. John's I spent many hours selecting the necessary volumes. When I reached Wesleyville my staff and I found that a spacious corner was not being utilized, so it did not take much time or money to create a library which all the senior and elementary pupils could use. With the many private donations, within a year a thousand books were on the shelves.

Our next move was to create a glee club. It was helpful that I had studied music for several years, and soon we had all the students of the upper grades joining a choir. In addition to providing entertainment the glee club earned money which we applied to various school programs. Other activities that we encouraged were athletics in one form or another and social and cultural events. As examples of the latter, periodically we held an "Open House" and a variety of exhibitions. Parents encouraged and supported the school's efforts to the point where it could be said that they were part of the whole process; without their cooperation we could never have achieved what we did.

Another project — one doubly welcome during the Depression years — was to provide a nutritious cocoa and milk drink ("cocomalt") during the recess period. I am not unduly sentimental, but there were times when I found it difficult to restrain my feelings when I saw what that simple drink meant to some of the pupils, many of whom came to school without having had any breakfast.

There were many instances of students who achieved excellence in spite of enormous difficulties. One example I shall call Frank.

Frank was a serious hunchback whose schooling had been impeded as much by the usual unfeeling reaction of his fellow students as by his physical deformity. He had received little help from his fellow students in the small school in which he had been enrolled, and after attending for a while he had given up entirely. When I heard of this I went to see the boy's father and discussed Frank's condition. Then I went to see the boy himself and as I talked with him I realized that, far from being mentally defective, he was probably above average in intelligence. I went back to the father and suggested that the boy return to school, and instead of continuing his Grade 8 come into my matriculation class. But the problem was that there was no money; most of the family were on relief. By chance, however, the job of lighting and maintaining the fires in the school's several potbellied stoves had become vacant, so I offered it to the boy. Far from this impeding him academically, he was able to devote the time he watched over the fires to his studies. When the results of the external examinations were published the following year, Frank had passed his matriculation with honours; he then went to summer school to get a grade and became an excellent teacher.

Unfortunately, Frank's deformity had been caused by spinal meningitis, and the disease had not been cured but was simply in abeyance. Several years later it struck once more, this time fatally. I could not attend his funeral, as I was at the University of Toronto at the time. But one day when I was in St. John's a stranger introduced himself to me, a teacher from Frank's school. He told me that Frank's last words had been: "Tell Mr. Rowe I never forgot him."

Many teachers can recall several episodes of that kind; here, perhaps, one more will suffice. Naboth Winsor was only nine years old when his father died in an accident. Naboth then lived with his grandmother and uncle. He was clearly above average in intelligence, but for some reason he had failed his Grade 11 year. This depressed him to the point that, taking into account the burden on his grandmother and uncle, he felt he should leave school altogether, and this he did. When I came to Wesleyville in 1936 he had been out of school three years, and was fishing at every opportunity. In our frequent chats, I gathered that his leaving school and thereby making any professional achievement impossible had been one of the great disappointments of his life. But when I suggested he should return to school, he still felt the whole plan would be impossible.

Fortunately, I was able to help him in three ways. First, through the fishery manager, whom I knew well, I was able to get Naboth's employment in the fish plant extended until mid-November instead of mid-October; this enabled him to use his earnings for clothes and other school expenses. Second, I was able to order his book supplies from St. John's and I allowed him to pay me when it was feasible. Third, I assisted him in his studies at night. (This was not always easy, as his place of work was some four miles away over a not very smooth road.) After mid-October Naboth was able to devote himself full-time to his matriculation.

In August, when the results came out, this young man, who had been three years out of school, received his honours matriculation diploma. After completing his matriculation in 1937, Naboth became a student minister. After several years in this capacity he went to university, graduating with high standing. One of the gratifying aspects of his career was that after ordination as a full-scale minister, he was invited to take over the United Church at Lewisporte. Here he spent seven years, a record at that time. And in 1977 Naboth Winsor attained one of Newfoundland's highest honours — President of the Newfoundland Conference of the United Church of Canada in Newfoundland.

9 Mount Allison and Grand Bank

The four years I spent at Wesleyville were among the most rewarding I had so far experienced at any school or community. We made many friends and our record was most gratifying. But even before the four-year period had terminated, there was a general restlessness in the air, probably to be attributed to World War II. For my own part, during these four years, I had continued my extramural studies, taking advantage of the excellent opportunities offered by Queen's University in Kingston and by Mount Allison in Sackville, New Brunswick, but I still lacked a degree, and would continue to do so as long as I failed to meet the residential requirements.

We now had two children, Fred, born in 1937, and Stanley, born in 1939. We lived comfortably and had built around us a small estate of household goods, but if I gave up my teaching salary our means would not be sufficient to meet our full needs for even the one year it would take to get my diploma. But we did have resources, so when I mentioned the possibility of going to Mount Allison, my wife favoured the idea more than when we were considering Memorial. We agreed that we would sell everything we didn't need. This included most of the furniture that we had acquired during the previous four years and most of my wife's extra clothes as well as her jewelry and other luxuries. The one item that we held onto was our ever-growing collection of books; these we crated and left with some of our Wesleyville friends until such time as we were once more settled.

That summer my wife took the children to Bonne Bay while I lectured at the Memorial Summer School, a practice we followed for a total of eight years. After this, I discontinued the lecturing to attend the summer session of the University of Toronto, but Edie and the boys continued to spend summers with her family in Bonne Bay for many years. The boys — we eventually had four, and no girls — experienced the kind of summers that might well be the envy of many a child. As the youngest female of the family, Edie enjoyed the traditional generosity accorded to the "pet" of the group both before and after her marriage; and that special treatment, it seemed, was extended to her boys as well. It should also be remembered that Edie's family still carried on a large and thriving business in spite of the economic and commercial vicissitudes.

For our two to four boys, the approach of the end of June meant the most magical of all experiences: a trip by train from St. John's to Deer Lake, a ride in their grandfather's Continental or Cadillac to Woody Point, and two full months of being pampered by their relatives.

The train ride itself was beyond description — a lovely parlour in the Pullman, the stops at scores of stations, the luxurious dining car with its uniformed waiters standing ready to cater to every whim. Why would anyone ever want to bother with a cramped airplane when there was such an alternative at hand? Then there was the ride in a luxury car for 42 miles through the mountains.

Once they arrived at Woody Point, there was the store to be inspected (and sampled); the Butt wharf with the tomcods and connors* looking up expectantly; a tour in their Uncle George's

* The connor is a species of fish much despised by wharf or stage-head anglers. Its size ranges from three to four inches to a foot and the thorns in its back are as obnoxious as its slimy skin. It is very difficult to hook, but is extremely skillful in preventing young tomcods from sampling the baited hook. In all, an objectionable creature.

lovely cabin cruiser; the official calls to be made on their buddies of former years; their utter joy when they heard that their cousin George had been given a .22-calibre rifle for his recent birthday; the cows and sheep and horses they had not seen since the previous year; the strawberries, raspberries, and other fruit not yet ripe enough to sample—is it any wonder that on the second day after their arrival, the doctor had to be hastily summoned to deal with the accumulations in one of the boys' stomachs?

The one place that never lost its attraction was the store, a deceptive building capable of carrying as much as $200,000 worth of stock at one time. The eldest daughter, Floss or Flossie (Florence), one of Newfoundland's outstanding businesswomen, was the executive head; but Edie's father, G. C. Butt, was nominally head of the firm, and he did not fail to invoke his control when occasion demanded. Once, Flossie had given a pair of long-rubbers to Fred, the eldest boy, and there was indignation among the other three over this obvious discrimination. But this did not last long. Within minutes the three had repaired to their unfailing source of help, who at once showed who was boss. "Floss, why haven't these boys got long-rubbers?" "Well, Father, I thought there was no need this fine summer day for the three younger ones to have long-rubbers." "Give a pair to each. They'll need them when the rain comes." End of discussion.*

After several summers of lecturing at Memorial, I registered at Mount Allison in September of 1940 with the intention of getting the necessary credits for my B.A. I needed, and proceeded to take, five full courses, two half courses, the full course of the Canadian Officers Training Corps (COTC) two nights a week, and a Latin matriculation course. This was unusual, as normally a year's program would consist of five full courses or the equivalent and nothing more; but in some strange way the dean, Dr. J. R. Tucker, missed finding out what I was doing for two or three weeks.

When he did discover it, he called me in to tell me I could not carry so heavy a load. This meant, of course, that I would not get my degree that year, a sickening thought after all the efforts I had made. I did my best to get him to change his mind but he was adamant. Finally, I thought up another approach. I said to him,

---

* Long-rubbers are a familiar sight in outport Newfoundland, where there is so much rain and fog. But to see four boys from age 5 to 12 all sporting new pairs of lovely long boots was something unusual. They were not wasted, however. In due time they were worn out trudging from home to school and back on the sidewalks of St. John's.

"Look at my Memorial record. There I was laden down but survived. Let me go on till Christmas and if by that time you feel I can't carry the load I'll accept your advice." To this Dr. Tucker agreed.

Within another month I was to have a broken leg, the result of a game of soccer; however, I kept on walking with the help of an iron heel, and come Christmas I did not refer the matter to Dr. Tucker nor did he bring it up. When the final results were released in the spring I had attained first-class honours in the five full courses and in one of the half courses. Also, during the year I had received the O. E. Smith Scholarship, an award given, I understood, on general merit.

In the spring of 1941 I had been invited to become principal of the largest United Church school outside St. John's, Grand Bank Academy. Though I only served in that capacity for one year, I think I should say a few words about Grand Bank.

This fishing town was well named, since it was relatively close to the Grand Banks, a great submarine plateau generally considered to be the richest fishery area in the world. To carry on the Bank fishery, several conditions had to be met. First, since the schooners would be out several hundred miles from land for weeks at a time, they had to be large enough to accommodate not only fishermen and their dories but food and supplies of all kinds. These same vessels also had to carry salt cod to the Caribbean, South America, and Mediterranean Europe; and since these ships had no power other than wind, it followed that they had to be strong and sturdy, capable at times of coping with the great Atlantic hurricanes.

In spite of all precautions, the mortality rate on the Grand Banks fishery was judged higher than that of any other occupation. This opinion has been held right up to modern times. For example, for decades Grand Bank, Fortune, Burin, Marystown, and Garnish, to name only a few, had more widows and orphans than any corresponding area in the world. It was, in fact, a portion of the earth's surface where everything seemed to conspire to make it unuseable: dense fog, the consequent danger of collision with other ships, helpless dories,* ice floes and icebergs, and above all storms and hurricanes beyond imagination except for those who actually experienced them.

---

* A banking schooner carried with it a number of dories—flat-bottomed boats crewed by several men. When the appropriate spot was reached the dories and their crew

Yet there were compensations. On the whole, general living conditions were probably among the highest in Newfoundland. There were excellent homes, and excellent schools by the standards of the day; a hospital was to be rebuilt; and a road system was designed to link the peninsular towns and, in time, to link those with the outside world.

Even though we had not quite recovered financially from our year at Mount Allison, my family and I enjoyed living in Grand Bank the year I was teaching there. Had I been 48 instead of 28, I would in all probability have spent the rest of my teaching life there. But though many things were attractive, the road system was not yet linked up with the outside world, and years of isolation lay ahead. This was especially unwelcome because I had what was at that time a Newfoundland rarity, a Bachelor degree, and a teaching reputation which was beginning to have island-wide implications. Rightly or wrongly, I felt that the world was my oyster. And so, when in June 1942 — the month our third son, Bill, was born — I received an offer from the Newfoundland government to become a Supervising Inspector of Schools, I accepted and by September I had assumed my duties.

The picture for me in 1942 was uncertain, to put it mildly. My supervisory "district" was a hodgepodge of educational shreds and tatters. It consisted of a portion of Trinity Centre, including all of Random Island; the Protestant portion of the Bonavista Peninsula (e.g. Bonavista, Catalina); the bottom portion of the Musgravetown area; just about all of Bonavista North (e.g. Wesleyville, Greenspond); the Strait Shore joining up Bonavista North with Gander Bay; and, in the event that there were other necessary areas unattended, any domain that officials within the department might allocate to me, including for example the Salvation Army portion of St. John's West.

In the district were 106 schools, of which the largest were Grand Bank, Wesleyville, and Bonavista, followed by a respectable number of three-, four-, or five-room schools; the large majority consisted of one-room, "sole-charge" schools. It was my duty to visit these schools regularly (usually spending half a day in a classroom), and then to discuss and plan the operation of the

---

were put in the water to jig or trawl fish from the dory. The dories were spread out over miles of water. Often fog made it difficult for dories to return to the mother ship. If a storm, gale, or hurricane struck the area, the dories and their crews were pretty helpless and as a rule could do little but wait until by luck or skill the schooner came upon them.

schools with the teachers, and when appropriate with the chairman of the board (usually a clergyman) or the full board.

At first, because of the war, there was considerable disruption. Appointments were made on a wartime basis, and no one was sure where he stood. The person I replaced had the option of coming back to his same position, so I was a temporary appointment even though common sense told me it was most likely that I would be retained. This uncertainty caused the most difficulty in trying to arrange housing. We were at that point well established in Grand Bank, but my supervisory district was scattered all over the east coast of Newfoundland. There was no road connection with the Burin Peninsula, on which Grand Bank was situated, and trips by coastal boats were long and inconvenient. But I could find no firm evidence that I would at some point be given the Burin district, the logical one because my wife and children were there and I was familiar with it.

I said little about this situation to my superiors, although it burned me up that such a stupid arrangement could not have been temporarily suspended, especially in view of the fact that for the whole year of my employment the Protestant sections of the Peninsula were completely ignored. The result for me was that I saw my wife and family only four times during the 12-month period. On one of these trips, the Christmas one, I was seven days and seven nights trying to reach Grand Bank. Very soon I made up my mind that at the first convenient time I would depart from the supervisory service forever.

To be fair, the system was not all bad. It provided a unifying factor even to the point of bringing to bear otherwise divisive church-educational groups; the almost constant travelling made the supervisors thoroughly familiar with conditions in the schools, as well as in the community; and the camaraderie that developed within the supervisory group no doubt promoted and encouraged the consolidating movement. However, one did have to learn to walk gingerly. In one community in my district an Anglican and a United Church school operated side by side in a state of near-collapse. Everywhere it was agreed that the two groups, of which one had two rooms and the other one or two rooms, should unite. Accordingly I called the respective boards together and enlisted their cooperation to build a single school with three or four classrooms. Things went well, but unfortunately the chairman of one of the boards had not been present at the meeting. When he heard of the action he immediately contacted his supervisors in the Department demanding that Rowe be told to mind his own business. The result? Two schools, one with one teacher, the other with three, were again built side by side, sharing a playground but nothing else. The two groups eventually unified but not until 25 years later. Undoubtedly, one of the reasons why the Protestant groups eventually took the bit in their own teeth a couple of decades later was this clear, and to some blatant, example of denominationalism gone wild.

At the risk of being considered flippant and facetious, one could say that the aim of most of the supervisors was simply to stay alive—literally. It is fact and not fantasy that in the 1930s and 1940s one could not travel around Newfoundland without running grave risks of one kind or another. Consider the following story. I am standing on the ice of the southwest arm of Random Sound, and the water is frozen for nearly two miles out. The local motorboat I am using is at the far end of the ice. My guide, his buddy, and I have to walk over the buckling ice to get to the boat. After some danger we are able to reach the shore where the boat is moored, a place out of sight of any person, and having gotten the engine started, we cross the arm—fortunately it is dead calm —to Little Hearts Ease. They put me ashore and set off for home again, having assured me they would pick me up the following morning. But they don't turn up. The reason? First of all, when they had gotten back to our point of departure the inch or two of ice had gone out the bay, so that the owners were able to get back to their wharf; but then during the night, a plank had simply dropped off the boat. The boat sank in seconds. Had the plank fallen off during the trip either way, all passengers would have lasted only the 15 or 20 minutes it takes to die from hypothermia in that kind of water.

Here is another story. I am travelling in the Cape Freels area, one of the roughest and most dangerous areas in eastern Canada, with almost unceasing fog to contend with. We have left Lumsden at noon in brilliant sunshine, but within half an hour one can barely see from one end of the boat to the other. Next, we discover the compass is not working. In short, we are lost. The owner can think of nothing better than to wander around in shallow water for the next four hours. Fortunately, for a few seconds there is a break in the fog. That has to be a western sighting! But in fact we are going east and the next land is France, 2000 miles away! My companion (a police officer) and I soon realize this and with difficulty finally convince the boat owner that we must do an about-face. We reach land just as a vicious storm is breaking, and ponder the fact that had we continued even for a half-hour to go east, we would have been caught by the storm — which our boat could not have survived.

One more. We are on Random Island, one of the largest islands making up Newfoundland. It is March and there has been a mild spell followed by several inches of fresh snow. We have to go to the far end of the island, about 14 miles. We set out in early morning. I take the precaution of carrying a stout stick about six feet long, something that makes my guide laugh. There is no road, so we must cross some of the numerous "ponds" (lakes) that dot every part of Newfoundland. When we are crossing a larger-than-usual pond it suddenly occurs to me that I have seen neither an entrance nor an exit to it. I stop and ask my guide to tell me where the brook that enters and leaves the pond is. He tells me there is none. I see a suspicious-looking configuration which induces me to back up slowly. In doing so I push my stick through the snow and discover hidden slob (soft ice). Had we broken through, as we undoubtedly would have if we had continued on that route for another few feet, we could not have lived more than 15 or 20 minutes, and the nearest help was five miles away. (After this it was not hard to convince my guide that he should at least take a strong stick the next time he was crossing ice.)

I have related these incidents not merely to illustrate the dangers we supervisors faced, but also as a warning against the sometimes needless risks taken by Newfoundlanders in their dealings with water. Again and again, nonswimmers drown because either there were no life jackets in the boat or the ones in the boat were not on the passengers. Several years ago three friends of mine went moose hunting in central Newfoundland. They carried three life jackets in their boat. The three jackets drifted ashore, but the men have never been found.

chapter

10 Curtis Academy and the University of Toronto

B y the spring of 1943 I puzzled over what the next step would be. Clearly, I could not carry on this way, seeing my family for only a few days three or four times a year. Furthermore, that family was increasing.

Fred had been born in 1937, Stanley (Bud) in 1939, Bill in 1942, and George would complete the family in 1944. Apart from other considerations, it was grossly unfair to my wife to leave her with such a burden. She did not complain, knowing that these arrangements were a routine part of life while a war was raging, but she detested it beyond measure. Anything that would change it would be welcome.

One aspect in which we were fortunate in the early years of our marriage was the quality of our housing. At Wesleyville, after months in an unsatisfactory house, we were lucky enough to find a first-class house, only four years old, whose owner had gone to St. John's to work; he agreed to rent his lovely house to us at the fairly standard rate of $6 a month, I believe. At Sackville, we were almost equally lucky, renting a portion of a large, near-palatial home, again for a nominal amount. Then, at Grand Bank, the leading businessman of the community rented us one of the three houses making up the managerial complex for something like $10 a month. Whatever our next move would be, we would again have to look for suitable housing, now for a larger family.

Some time in May I visited St. John's after finishing my spring trip through the district, boarding with a most estimable family, the Hoddinotts. While we were having breakfast, one of the daughters asked me whether I had heard of the new school the United Church was building in the west end of the city. Strangely enough, I had not heard anything about it, probably because I had had to spend so much time travelling. I made further enquiries and then arranged an interview with a St. John's businessman, Mr. A. E. Parkins, who was the secretary-treasurer of the United Church School Board in St. John's. The net result of the interview was that Mr. Parkins invited me to meet the full board.

It was an interesting meeting, with just about the full board present. Apart from the four United Church clergymen who were ex officio members of the board, most of the well-known business leaders of St. John's were present: e.g. H. J. Russell, C. C. Pratt, Harold Macpherson, H. Clyde Lake, James Herder, L. C. Currie, Harold Luscombe, George G. Crosbie, Daniel Pelley, and L. R. Curtis. We had a long discussion and when I walked out I was principal of the new school being built. This institution was later named Curtis Academy, after the Rev. Dr. Levi Curtis, the famous clergyman and educator who had been head of the Methodist and United Church for over 40 years.

Having secured a position in St. John's, I had to find a place to live there, but in 1943 housing was almost totally unavailable. It was a casual encounter on LeMarchant Road with a lady whom I had met only once, that elicited from her the news that a well-to-do couple living on Prince of Wales Street were planning to sell their excellent four-bedroom house. I thanked the acquaintance and then probably broke another record in reaching the couple's home. I spoke to the wife. Yes, they were thinking of selling; yes, she would be glad to show me around (Edie was in Bonne Bay); no, she had not committed herself with some other person; yes, they would wait a couple of days to give me a chance to make arrangements. Now, at the moment I did not have a dollar to my name. But I did not tell her this, for what I did have was a school board more than half of whose individual members could have bought me a house. Within a day we had bought the house on a four-percent mortgage. And so, during the five years that I was principal of Curtis Academy, we had first-class accommodations in a home of our own.

We opened Curtis in September 1943 while it was still only about half done. Curtis took the place of a wooden, rat-ridden firetrap known as Centennial Hall, but we had more than twice as many students as the old school had accommodated. The great movement of centralization had already started in St. John's as in other places, and thousands of children were looking for schools.

As more classrooms at Curtis were completed we moved the pupils into them, but even with that there was gross overcrowding, not just in Curtis but in every large school system in the country. By 1946, with well over 1000 students, Curtis had the largest registration in Newfoundland. Under the old school system, students requiring matriculation were told they could go to Prince of Wales College. In practice, this had never really worked. Pupils who reached Grade 10 (and they were a small number) simply left school; the irony of this was that a student living in Grand Bank or Carbonear had a far better chance to obtain a Grade 11 matriculation than did the majority of the St. John's students who came from the "lower middle class" and "lower class," to use an objectionable terminology.

The Prince of Wales board, as distinct from the United Church board, wanted to perpetuate the old system, but a number of us opposed it vehemently and eventually succeeding in getting the United Church Conference (the annual meeting of the ministers) to stand behind our board, both in the matter of grades and in that of consolidating the two United Church boards, the College Board and the St. John's Board. Eventually the two boards combined to form one as the Anglican and Roman Catholic had done.* The official title of the St. John's board is Avalon Consolidated School Board.

---

* Later the three largest Protestant boards joined together to form a single system.

Curtis was a new school, I was a new principal, and fewer than half of the pupils had ever attended a large school — one-third or more had come from the outports, from schools big and small (mostly small) and they had totally mixed backgrounds. I saw this at once as a golden opportunity to introduce a series of programs that could, I hoped, revolutionize not just the curriculum but the lives of the children, who now found themselves in a brand new world.

But there was a war on and we had to struggle to get materials and equipment amid the competition that war creates. I had to fight to get even the basic equipment for the classrooms. That competition extended to staff, as there was a demand for both men and women, especially the former, for the war. After all, one cannot recruit several thousand young people from a restricted environment such as Newfoundland's and not create serious repercussions.

By pointing out, among other things, that we would not achieve much if when victory came we found ourselves with a majority of our young people wallowing in illiteracy and ignorance, we gradually acquired the basic necessities: blackboards, seats, desks, science equipment for the laboratories, household science items, music equipment, a library, and audiovisual equipment. In every area without exception we started from nothing and went on to create a civilized academic and cultural environment.

By far the most revolutionary program was the school prefect system, which we established early — in 1943. I am sure that many who read that sentence will say, "What's Rowe talking about? We had prefects in our school 50 years ago. There's nothing new in that." There was, however, something very new in the Curtis system, as any former student would attest: the high school student body elected all the prefects by private vote. There was one important exception: the principal reserved the right to appoint the two chief prefects from the group elected. But in the five years that I served at Curtis, never once did I exercise that right, for the simple reason that there was no need to. When the time came for prefects to be installed I simply passed over my prerogative to the senior students, who went ahead and selected the head prefects by democratic process. Thereafter, of course, the prefects controlled or administered whole sections of school activity. As new services were added to the school's program, the prefects took over; the outdoor skating rink and the beautiful library were examples. I have talked with many former student-prefects, and when I have asked them what aspect of life at Curtis they liked most, almost invariably the answer has been "the prefect system."

The verve and enthusiasm were not confined to the student body, important as that was. In retrospect it almost seems as if the teachers at all levels were determined not to be outdone by the students. What with plans for plays, concerts, operettas, open houses, exhibitions, home and school joint ventures, etc., it was obviously impossible for teachers to attend to this relatively huge school without assuming after-hours work of one kind or another; but never in the five years did I hear a single complaint.

Curtis Academy is now gone, the victim, apparently, of wanton arson by teenagers who had never legally been within its walls.* Gone is that beautiful auditorium, gone the massive concrete walls, gone the lovely classrooms, the hundreds of pictures on the staff room walls, the spotless washrooms, and all the other things that made it one of the great schools of Newfoundland. But the memories are there. A few years ago, the former students of Curtis held their first reunion and invited me to be their guest speaker. I expected the usual number that one sees or hears about at such reunions, a few hundred coming together to make a satisfying evening, with the usual speakers, etc. But when I entered the auditorium I was flabbergasted. Here was one of the biggest Newfoundland gatherings of its kind ever to come together — so many, indeed, that the largest hall in St. John's could not accommodate them and two evenings were required. These beautiful women, these handsome men, the businessmen, lawyers, teachers, doctors, politicians, technicians, underwriters — all had known in their hearts that this great school could not be destroyed by vandalic acts, that it would live on in our memories forever.

The years from 1943 to 1948 were among the busiest of my life, largely due to my involvement in the creation and operation of Curtis Academy. As a rule, principals and teachers derived some rest from the year's work during the summer holidays, but two factors interfered in this: the practice of paying us only for the ten months of the year during which the schools were open and the need for us to use the summer months to improve our academic standing. Thus, the summer months, far from improving our

---

* Curtis Academy was only one of the half-dozen or so schools that suffered arson, successful or attempted.

financial condition, actually made things tougher as we sought the money, one way or another, to take advantage of what universities were offering in the academic field.

My financial burdens were lightened somewhat by the fact that by the late 1930s I had virtually become an unofficial member of the summer school staff at Memorial College; I lectured there in English and Education each summer from 1938 to 1946. These summers were both pleasant and rewarding. However, as time wore on, it became increasing clear that if I were to gain maximum benefit from the summer season, I too would have to discontinue these lectures in favour of my studies. I became increasingly aware that, apart from anything else, academic competition alone demanded that I join the ranks of students at the summer sessions of the university.

The demand for summer courses became stronger as World War II came to an end and thousands of discharged veterans sought to catch up on time lost during the war; the situation was made more intense by the various programs for veterans' aid offered by the Newfoundland government. Nevertheless, with thousands of other students, I took some advantage of summer sessions to gain improvements in one way or another. I remember that one of the courses I took consisted of what we would today call French immersion; another summer I registered in a navigation course.

By 1947 I had spent five academic years at work which was most pleasurable, but which had taken a great deal out of me. It had become clear that apart from my need to pursue studies, the time had come for me to break away, at least temporarily, from the burdens of work that almost literally bent me down from day to day. I decided that the best thing would be for me to begin actively studying year-round, including the summer, for my pedagogy degree with the University of Toronto, while still engaging in extramural studies. I had had earlier opportunities to carry on summer studies there, but had been deterred by a growing family and the need to use the work break to supplement my income. Moreover, there had been the problem of the residential requirements at that institution.*

---

* Like most other universities, the University of Toronto, while supporting summer studies as much as possible, continued to give major importance to year-round students. St. John's suffered from this policy, as did many other cities and towns in Canada.

I asked my school board for a leave of absence, which they granted without hesitation. I should also say that they offered me substantial and generous salary increases if I would stay on, increases that would have made me the highest-paid principal in Newfoundland. I admit I was tempted, but not for long.

Of course, we came up against the housing problem once more. The war was not long over; everywhere people were looking for apartments and homes, and no one would rent to families with four husky boys and a maid. What was the solution? At first, nothing. Then, while I was relaxing one evening, an idea struck like a bolt of lightning. My relatives by marriage, the Colbournes, were among Toronto's leading builders. Also, we had a home in St. John's, which was worth money. Why not sell our house and engage Colbourne Construction to build another for us? No sooner said than done. And so during my sojourn at the University of Toronto my family lived in a three-bedroom brick home with every possible convenience, e.g. front and back lawns, a full-size basement with furnace, a living room, a dining room, a kitchen with the usual installations, and three bedrooms.

Meanwhile, another factor entered the picture — Confederation.

THE NEWFOUNDLAND POLITICIAN 1949–1972

chapter
11 *Confederation*

*B*ack in 1934, when for all practical purposes Newfoundland had gone broke, the British parliament, urged on by Newfoundland itself, had suspended the right to self-government which, in common with the other dominions, we had enjoyed for some years. At the time, we were assured that if Newfoundland once more became self-supporting Britain would have no hesitation in restoring the status of self-government, provided we indicated a favourable attitude to such a restoration. So it was that during the period from 1934 to 1949, dominion status was set aside and Newfoundland was governed by the Commission of Government.

As World War II dragged on, it became clear that due to the impact of the demand for Newfoundland products such as fish, iron, and paper, the presence of great American bases, and the consequent nearly full-time employment, Newfoundland was once again almost self-supporting for the first time since World War I.

There were, however, some imponderables: What would happen once the war ended and the bases closed down? Would the Newfoundland economy still be able to support itself, and would there be sufficient momentum in the economy to look after not just the returned veterans but the rapidly increasing population as well? No one knew the answer to these questions. However, there were many who feared that Newfoundland's economy was ephemeral — that the economic hardships that had occurred after the cessation of previous wars would inevitably happen again. Those who held such fears felt that the term "self-supporting" was somewhat meaningless, and that the clause respecting self-government was no guarantee of any permanent economic prosperity. In short, they felt that once the war was over Newfoundland could look forward to nothing but poverty and hardship, as it had at the end of World War I. The only difference would be that Newfoundland's population would be much larger than it had been a few decades before, making the problem all' the greater.

This whole matter was one of great concern to Great Britain, who had been forced to come to Newfoundland's aid in the 1930s. The urgency of the problem may be gauged by the fact that when the outcome of World War II was still far from a certainty, Clement Atlee — later to become prime minister of Britain — and several other British parliamentarians deemed it advisable to come out to Newfoundland to evaluate the situation.

To Atlee's credit, he did not mince words or try to delude the Newfoundland people in any way. He foresaw the likelihood that once the war was over it would be only a matter of time before Newfoundland was again bankrupt and in need of help from Britain. Atlee also knew that Britain would not be able to help as before because Britain itself would be in a state of near-bankruptcy. This amounted to a clear warning that if Newfoundland demanded a return to self-government and received it, Britain could not be counted on to rush to the rescue, and that Newfoundland should be giving thought to other measures while the time was still propitious.

What other measures were there? With Britain out of the picture there appeared to be two: union with Canada on a provincial basis, or a union of some kind with the United States.

This second choice was one that both Canada and Britain looked upon with some disquiet. World War II had already shown the importance of Newfoundland from the strategic viewpoint. In addition, its economic fragility could not be ignored. While it was true that the United States and Canada were friends, this happy state of affairs could not always be counted on; even countries with strong political ties could find themselves at odds economically. One thing was certain: once a foreign military body became established on the Island of Newfoundland, dislodging it would be a major enterprise.

Yet the prospect of union between Canada and Newfoundland was for different reasons equally obnoxious to many Newfoundlanders. Such a union had been considered on several previous occasions, notably in the 1860s, when under a masterful political leader the confederates had been thoroughly defeated by arguments that could still be considered valid for the 1940s. Perhaps the most potent of these was the argument that in any union with Canada Newfoundland might very well become more of a vassal than a province.

By 1945 two loose but distinct groups had emerged, the confederates and the anticonfederates. The former group was composed mostly of political liberals, teachers, fishermen, loggers, lower-paid civil servants, trade unionists, and religious evangels; it was led by Joseph R. Smallwood, a former farmer, journalist, and writer with immense powers of debate. The latter group was composed of mercantile and professional groups and east-coast Roman Catholics; the anticonfederates did not have anyone with the rhetorical skills that Smallwood could invoke and was left without an effective leader during most of the campaign.

When the Confederation issue became hot, I was still principal at Curtis Academy. At first I took little active part in the debate, but at no time did I attempt to disguise my feelings—I was in favour of joining Canada, as my parents had been and indeed most of the people of Lewisporte.

There were a number of reasons for the Lewisporte bias toward Confederation. First, there was the tendency of the Lewisporte people to migrate to Toronto in search of work and education. Second, the people of Lewisporte were mostly members of the United Church, whose headquarters were in Toronto; and most of the Church literature was printed there by Ryerson Press, their official publisher. Third, most Lewisporte people living in Toronto returned home periodically, inevitably displaying signs of the economic difference between Lewisporte and Toronto; moreover, when times were bad at home, the Toronto relatives were always ready to send help in the form of clothing or money. Thus the people of Lewisporte could visualize good times in their future if Confederation came about.

I played my first active role in the Confederation issue when I took part in debates at what was then Newfoundland's best-known debating forum, the Methodist College Literary Institute; on several occasions I expressed myself volubly and forcefully. Of course, I was careful not to allow my feelings regarding Confederation to become a political football in the school, but I felt that as a private individual I should be able to express myself on public matters without reservations.

This fact did not escape the attention of a large number of Newfoundland teachers who shared my sentiments. Up to then most of these teachers had apparently taken cognizance of the fact that, especially in the larger centres, school boards were made up of clergymen and well-to-do businessmen who were mostly opposed to Confederation; for whatever reason, a majority of the teachers had been extremely reticent when it came to expressing themselves on the Confederation issue. But as time went on this began to change. As the founding president of the St. John's branch of the Newfoundland Teachers' Association I was helping to develop a number of programs for the branch which, while not blatantly political, encouraged teachers to speak out frankly on matters of public interest. More and more of the Protestant teachers — including those in the larger centres — began to be willing to express themselves openly. As for the Roman Catholic teachers in the large centres, the situation was not quite the same with them, for the simple reason that many were members of religious teaching orders and were not used to speaking out in controversial political matters.

On Saturday, February 26, 1948, an announcement was made that a formation meeting of the confederates was to be held in the Newfoundland Hotel. I attended, and to my surprise I found myself elected, along with Dr. Solomon Whiteway of Normal School fame and one or two others, a vice-president of the St. John's branch. This from time to time gave me opportunities to participate in and speak at public meetings — and in addition to speak on the radio, a medium which was becoming increasingly powerful in the Confederation controversy. Apparently these actions as well affected a large number of teachers who felt that if Rowe, the president of the St. John's branch of the Newfoundland Teachers' Association and principal of the largest school in the country, could speak out with impunity, they could do the same.

During the academic years 1946-1948, I continued to support Confederation; and prior to my decision to resign from Curtis and move to Toronto I had met with Smallwood, who to my pleasure had invited me to enter his first cabinet. He expected this cabinet to be in existence in the spring or summer of 1948. Though this would have upset my plans to attend university, I did not reject his offer immediately because the time element was somewhat uncertain. But eventually he told me that the new government — if the Confederation movement was successful — would be in force not later than July or August 1948, so I reluctantly had to refuse his offer.*

As it happened, the referenda were not held until July of 1948 and the new government was not formed until April 1949, just as I was completing my residential requirements in Toronto and thinking about my thesis. At this point I had a serious decision to make regarding my career. Several prospects were open: to return to Curtis, where the board was still holding open the principalship for me, to remain in Toronto and continue to build up a career in the field of education, or to move to the United States, where the tremendous upsurge in wartime and postwar development was just at its peak.

I decided to return to Newfoundland. If, in the referenda, Confederation had lost, I had determined not to return to Newfoundland — more in consideration of the welfare of my family than anything else. But with Confederation a certainty it had become obvious that job opportunities would be very plentiful. We put our Toronto house up for sale, made a substantial profit, and returned to St. John's — where once more a stroke of luck gave us first chance at an excellent home, one we would keep for the next 13 years.

My interest in active politics, which had diminished somewhat during my sojourn in Toronto, was stimulated once more, and this fact seemed to please the new premier. There was now no opening in the Cabinet, but that did not deter Smallwood very long, for the new government included several portfolios that required the services of senior officials.

One area in which most Newfoundlanders were deeply interested was public welfare. The new minister of this department was to be Dr. H. L. Pottle — previously Commissioner of Public Health and Welfare — under whose supervision I had worked for a year or so in the Department of Education while I was a supervis-

---

* Smallwood then committed himself to Sam Hefferton, a respected and dedicated teacher.

ing inspector. Also, while I was not a fully trained sociologist, many of my university courses had been in the general welfare field. With all this in mind, Smallwood and Pottle developed the idea that I should be the government's first Deputy Minister of Public Welfare. However, the Premier made it quite clear that he would expect me to move into the Cabinet at the first opportunity; Pottle concurred. And so in June 1949 I took up the responsibility, under the direction of Dr. Pottle, of helping to build what was to become, in the minds of many welfare people across Canada, one of the country's most innovative and pioneering welfare systems.

Before 1949, welfare, in the true sense of the word, was practically nonexistent in Newfoundland. But under the Smallwood government measure after measure of social reform was introduced, with the lot of the Newfoundland people improving in proportion. The social reforms were not all province-based, of course; some of the most notable — unemployment insurance, family allowance, old age security, and veterans' allowance — were completely federal; without the federal presence much of the welfare provided since 1949 would not have been possible. But this should not lead one to minimize or derogate the provincial contribution.

One noticeable aspect of welfare during the period since 1949 has been the improvement in physical conditions. Perhaps the two most obvious examples of this are the elimination of most poor and slipshod housing and the general healthy appearance of Newfoundland children.

One of the earliest discoveries affecting my own work as Deputy Minister was the colossal ignorance of so many Newfoundland people about welfare matters, especially regarding new programs.* This lack of correct information revealed itself in many ways, the most obvious of which was the number and nature of the letters received at the new Department. For week after week the number addressed to me personally ranged around 400, and most of these evinced a great unawareness of the social system. Other welfare personnel could cite similar figures.

One partial solution that occurred to me was to start a weekly radio show devoted entirely to welfare matters. The government agreed to authorize me to sponsor such a program, and within a

---

* During the early months of Confederation, the Newfoundland government assisted the Canadian government in implementing new welfare legislation.

few weeks it was clear that it was a complete success. On this program I drew from many of the letters (anonymously, of course) questions that would be of interest to hundreds of present and potential recipients of the newly available social services. Among the major topics were old age security, workmen's compensation, dependents' allowance, family allowance, mother's allowance, and veterans' allowance.

The problem of conveying information plagued not merely the welfare authorities but also all types of private organizations such as churches and service clubs. Examples of the latter were, to name only a few, the Rotary, Kiwanis, Lions, Kinsmen, and the Junior Chamber of Commerce. Traditionally, each club periodically took on one or more major projects: assisting crippled children, building parks and swimming pools, instituting music festivals, providing scholarships, helping underprivileged children, and countless other projects big and small. Much of Newfoundland's welfare work — a disproportionally large amount considering the nature and problems of the population and the size of most service organizations — was done privately in this manner. The Department was more than willing to supply the informational needs of these organizations. My feeling is that the various churches, clubs, and other groups have never been given full credit for all they have done in the welfare field.

chapter

12 *Labrador*

*I*n the fall of 1951, Mr. Smallwood decided to call a general
election. Since the sitting member for Labrador, Harold Hor-
wood, had indicated his intention of withdrawing from active politics, this could have provided the opening for me that Smallwood
desired; however, for a number of reasons he decided to select
one of the Labrador businessmen to run in that district and to
hold me back for another opening where, so he said, my talents
could be better employed.

What he apparently underestimated was my popularity among
the Labrador people. No sooner was Smallwood's decision made
public than there was a small rebellion with leaders of the Moravian Mission, the heads of the Grenfell Mission, and some other
mercantile and religious spokesmen importuning Smallwood to
run Fred Rowe. Smallwood now found himself on the horns of a
very serious dilemma, since he could not very well change his
mind just then. However, the election call coming late in 1951
and the weather conditions being most inauspicious that fall, he
was given the chance to postpone the Labrador election. This
meant that the election for that district could not be held until

1952, by which time support for me had reached an almost unanimous point.

The election was finally called for July 1952. When nomination day arrived, there was no one to oppose my being elected by acclamation, with all of Labrador as my district. Therefore, for the next four years I represented Labrador and sat in the Cabinet as Minister of Mines and Resources.*

As the member for Labrador, the situation that concerned me most was the condition of the Indians in the area around North West River and Davis Inlet. Indeed, following my first visit my concern led me to meet with several of the local leaders — Rev. F. W. Peacock, Dr. Anthony Paddon, Rev. Father Cyr, Dr. Charles Curtis, and Dr. Gordon Thomas — and with the civil service authorities responsible for the welfare of the Indians. To my horror, virtually all these people were of the opinion that these natives were on the way to extinction. Moreover, the evidence was clear that the Inuit were also in a precarious position.

When I became Labrador's government representative, I had not yet begun the research that led to my book *Extinction: The Beothuks of Newfoundland*. However, I had grown up in an area where tuberculosis was rampant. I knew what TB looked like, and I did not need anyone to tell me that the Indians of northern Labrador were on the road to extinction.

But for the heroic measures taken by the government of Newfoundland, the government of Canada, the Moravian Mission, the Catholic Church, the United Church, and the International Grenfell Association in conjunction with the member for the district, we would today most probably be talking about another extinct race. While perhaps one should not speak too optimistically about the changes that continue to take place in the lives of the Indians and Inuit of Labrador, most certainly their lives and cultures have been preserved for decades to come.

As minister and member for various portfolios and districts, I have frequently been asked what were my most satisfying experiences. The preservation of the Naskapi and Montagnais Indians was perhaps the most deeply significant of all. It is a role for which I have never refrained from taking some credit. It has been a source of continuing gratification to me that Labrador leaders

---

* Later, in the electoral division of 1956, Labrador was divided into Labrador North and Labrador South.

such as Dr. Paddon and Dr. Peacock have been generous enough to acknowledge my role.

But there have been other satisfying experiences, and among them is the story of Happy Valley.

When I arrived at Goose Airport in 1952 on my first visit to Labrador, I was naturally interested and intrigued by this great territory where my father had spent so much of his life. As the member for the district and a cabinet minister, I was extended every possible courtesy by the authorities, and right away I was enthralled, almost amazed, by the great air base being operated by the American and Canadian governments.

As the officials drove me around, I asked about the Hamilton River (later renamed the Churchill River), about which I had heard so much and, curiously enough, in some respects so little. In time I was taken down to view it. Travelling in a military vehicle over a gravel road built by the bases, I saw among the bank of that great river, stretching for a mile or more, shacks and houses capable of accommodating perhaps 600 or 700 settlers.

Since this was part of the base concession, I was naturally curious about this shantytown and made further inquiries. Essentially, I ascertained that these people were illegal settlers on a portion of base property called Happy Valley about five miles from the base townsite at Goose Bay. They were almost entirely Newfoundlanders, some from the Island, others from coastal Labrador.

The base authorities found themselves in an ambivalent position regarding these settlers. Goose, at the time, was the second-largest and the fastest-growing air base in the world.* All over the area, there were work projects and everywhere there was a demand for workers, especially skilled artisans. In other words, the base needed the Happy Valley residents. However, the authorities did not want a permanent settlement to grow up only four or five miles from an important strategic base at a time when the Cold War could escalate into a major war within minutes.

As I looked into this matter further, I discovered a number of incredible anomalies. I found that the Happy Valley settlers had no rights whatsoever: no one had title to land, no one could own a vehicle, no commercial enterprise could be undertaken, and no store could be built. But the base did allow one concession: they would provide an open truck to transport a woman, and where

---

* The largest being the O'Hare in Chicago.

necessary her child or children, to the Hudson's Bay store at Goose Bay to do her shopping. That this might be in the middle of February with the temperature − 20° or − 30° F was not considered to be very important.

Some of the families got together to form a school and church, and some tried to get a drinking water supply by driving an artesian well into the sand; but of other sanitary services there were none. If few residents complained, it was for the simple reason that they were employed — at very good wages — by the base, and did not want to risk being ejected, as had happened to some previous troublemakers.

I found the situation unbelievable and unacceptable, so at the earliest opportunity I made arrangements to meet with the base colonels. Our conversation went along these lines:

Rowe: I was surprised to find six or seven hundred people settled in your territory on the river bank. What are they doing there?
Col.: These are illegal settlers on our base. We have turned away a great many of them and we plan to turn them all away in time.
Rowe: As far as I can see most of them are working. That means, I suppose, that you need them?
Col.: Well, yes. But we don't want them stuck so near our base. After all, things are pretty tense and we could have a war at any minute. We wouldn't want to evacuate six or seven hundred people on short notice.
Rowe: Why not?
Col.: Well, as I've already said, we're turning a lot away.
Rowe: What's the difference between Happy Valley and St. John's? At St. John's we have nearly a hundred thousand people, all of whom would be victims of a war. Are you suggesting we should move all St. John's and let Pepperrell stay there for the war?

And what about Argentia? If a war starts, would evacuating thousands of people from Argentia be any different from Happy Valley?

And what about Harmon Field? Do we evacuate the fifteen thousand there?

In short, what is the difference between Happy Valley and any of the other great bases that are next door to large population centres?
Col.: Well, it's our base and we intend to keep it as such.
Rowe: How do you justify depriving these Canadian citizens of their basic rights? For example, if Mrs. Hounsell wants a pair of shoes or a reel of cotton in the middle of the winter, how does she get it?
Col.: She can go up on one of our trucks and buy whatever she wants.
Rowe: Five miles away?

Col.:   Nobody makes her go.

Rowe: What about anything else?

Col.:   She can go up there for anything else.

Rowe: Can Mr. Roberts, for example, buy and operate a motorcar?

Col.:   No.

Rowe: Can the Hudson's Bay Company build a store here?

Col: No.

Rowe: Colonel, this situation is intolerable. Are you telling me that hundreds of Canadian citizens are being deprived of their basic rights because you say so?

Col.:   (now angry) Dr. Rowe, this is our territory. We will operate this goddamn place as we think it should be, politicians or no politicians.

Rowe: Colonel, I have a piece of news for you. You may not like it but this country—which includes Labrador—is under the government of Newfoundland and Labrador. That goddamn bunch of politicians are running it. You will hear from me again. Good day!

After reporting the situation to Premier Smallwood in St. John's, and getting his agreement on the course of action to be taken, I took off for Ottawa to meet with the Honourable Brooke Claxton,* the Minister of National Defence.

Claxton had with him his deputy minister, the Honourable Charles M. Drury—a former military figure in World War II— and at this point I was ready to assume that Drury would be a kissing cousin to the Goose Bay colonels. Apparently this was the case; at any rate, after listening very briefly, Claxton and Drury decided to put this Newfoundland upstart Rowe in his place. However, I did not have the time to be patted on the back and told, "Go home, Daddy will look after things for you."

Standing up, I gradually and literally pushed Claxton into the corner. I then proceeded to describe approximately as follows the roster of inequalities in effect in Happy Valley:

Rowe: Here you have a group of law-abiding, hard-working individuals who want nothing more than a chance to earn a living. You give them that right when it suits you, and kick them out whenever you want to.

Mr. Claxton, I am a Liberal, as you are. If the situation in Happy Valley is allowed to continue I will blast your name and your deputy's across Canada. I will invite the media to come into Happy Valley and see for themselves. I hesitate to do this, as we are political colleagues, but I will not allow that to interfere.

---

* Possibly the most popular cabinet minister in Ottawa.

Your name, and incidentally that of the party, will be mud across
Canada — all because of your willingness to allow your deputy and a
number of civil servants to run the base in an unnecessarily stupid
way, in the process treating Newfoundlanders as third-class citizens.
Claxton: (visibly disturbed) What do you recommend?
Rowe: Given the authority, the Hudson's Bay Company can begin
within the week to build at Happy Valley a first-class store
unequalled in eastern Canada. These people should have the right to
own and operate a car, the same right that other Canadians and
Newfoundlanders enjoy.

But what about the land question? Having discussed this with
Hudson's Bay Company leaders, I was in a position to make a
substantive recommendation to Claxton. Since the Goose Bay
base had far more space than the bases on the Island of Newfoundland, why not select a portion of the land concession and
return it to the Crown? The Crown could then make land grants
to those already living on the land or to those wishing to live
there. Claxton heard me out, and when I had finished he thought
at some length. He then said to me:

> I am disturbed to hear what you have had to say. Something has
> to be done. I am going to the prime ministers' conference in Lon-
> don next week and I shall ask our pilot to go by way of Goose,
> rather than Gander, so that I may see at first hand what condi-
> tions are like. The idea of granting land lots appeals to me.

Claxton, one of nature's gentlemen, did in fact make a point of
viewing the Goose Bay situation at first hand, and the most
immediate result was the construction of a great Hudson's Bay
store. Within ten years, Happy Valley became one of the most
thriving towns in Newfoundland. Today the twin townships of
Happy Valley-Goose Bay — the two are often yoked thus — are
among the most prosperous in the entire province. The residents
hold title to their own land and have enjoyed for years all the
rights that other Canadian citizens have always enjoyed.

In Labrador, a land replete with interesting characters, the
most interesting to me was a man named Jacob Penny.

Jacob was descended from the Pennys of the north shore of
Conception Bay. As a very young man he settled in Williams Har-
bour, near Port Hope Simpson on the Alexis Bay and River in
Labrador. Like many other fishermen in Labrador, Uncle Jacob
Penny lived on the coast (Williams Harbour) during the fishing

season and moved some 20 miles "in the country" during the winter.

He was about five feet, two inches in height and I would guess he weighed around 320 pounds. When I first met him I was foolish enough to think that much that made up the weight of this man-mountain was ordinary fat. However, I realized my mistake when I happened to squeeze his arm as hard as I could one day while we were "foolin' around." What I felt—through several layers of clothing—was obviously concrete or steel. One thing was certain, there was no extra flesh.

On several occasions as my family and I approached Williams Harbour with the intent to go inland to Port Hope Simpson, Uncle Jacob came alongside and boarded our boat (often the *Bonnie Nell*) just to be with us on the run, leaving his own large boat to the crew—who were all, I believe, members of his own family.*

It was on such excursion that the subject of summer clothes came up. On the run up to Port Hope Simpson, with the temperature around 100° F, I had stripped off and was lying on the cabin roof of the *Bonnie Nell* getting one of the best suntans of my life.† But after a while I noticed that Uncle Jacob was showing signs of distress, so I went back to offer my advice. "Uncle Jacob," I said, "I think you should take off some of those clothes you have on." He agreed, and loosened up some of his clothing.

That day he had on two suits of heavy woollen underwear, two heavy work shirts, and two jackets. How he had managed to survive in such temperatures dressed like that I never did find out. (I ought to mention, however, that when Uncle Jacob had gone out that morning in the cool hours before daylight to pull his traps, he had likely not been overdressed.)

Uncle Jacob was not just a fisherman. During the winter he cut enormous logs and pulpwood, and besides trapping and hunting rabbits, porcupine, beaver, and caribou for food, he was also a

---

* My regular summer visit to the district was made on several occasions by hiring the abovementioned Twillingate Hospital boat. She was a stalwart vessel, about 48 feet long. I had reason to be thankful for this once when, crossing the Strait of Belle Isle, we encountered a vicious storm in which a less strong boat would very likely have foundered. My feelings can best be imagined when it is noted that my wife and my two younger sons, Bill and George, were with me at the time.

† Contrary to what many believe, the river mouths and the long indrafts of Labrador can produce summer temperatures far higher than anything to be found around the Island of Newfoundland. I think the two hottest days I have ever experienced were both in Labrador—one at North West River and one at Goose Airport.

fur trapper and went after wolf, mink, lynx, weasel, and black bear. He was also an entrepreneur, involved in a variety of mercantile and commercial activities. These enterprises brought him to St. John's from time to time where he called at our home — always a welcome visitor.

Uncle Jacob loved dark rum, and whenever he called on us I made sure we had a good supply of his favourite beverage. I had no hesitancy in letting him have several hefty drinks, since I had never seen him under the influence. I assumed that even heavy consumption would have little effect on him because his body was so huge that the alcohol became absorbed in short order.

However, there was one occasion, while I was in Labrador, that was an exception. After spending the night a few miles outside Williams Harbour, at daybreak I asked the skipper to start in. We arrived sometime before 5 a.m. To my utter astonishment we found ourselves in what looked to be an abandoned community. Not a person was visible; no smoke rose from the chimneys; and not a motorboat or skiff was to be seen or heard. But this unnatural calm lasted only a short time. Within minutes there was a bedlam of motorboats as the men returned from their fishing traps, and shortly the *Bonnie Nell* was surrounded by every boat in the harbour.

After greeting all my friends I told them I would meet them at Uncle Jacob's house after I had had a cup of tea, and went to have a chat with Jacob on his stage.

Everyone knew what the "talk" with Uncle Jacob meant but no one begrudged him a drink or two on a fine cold morning. I had with me a bottle of Lemonhard about one-third full. I had never taken a drink in the morning in my life, but I invited Jacob to drink as much as he liked. Within 20 minutes or so he had demolished the Lemonhard.

As we walked up the path from his stage to his house, Uncle Jacob not only became more voluble, but, to my consternation, he started to sway a little. By now some of the other villagers were beginning to come out, so I quickly got Jacob into his house and hidden, I hoped, from prying eyes.*

When we got into the large kitchen — where Mrs. Penny and one or two of her daughters were busy getting together a huge

---

* I had always been cautious with alcohol, and was especially cautious now that I was in public life. The last thing I needed as a practising politician was a charge that Rowe was going around making his constituents drunk.

breakfast of ham and eggs—Uncle Jacob wanted to talk. I suggested we go to the "inside" room where we would be alone and he agreed.

There were several chairs in the room—one, very large and highly strengthened, was obviously Jacob's. After giving me a gentle push, which almost knocked me against the wall, he sat himself down with such force and weight that the huge chair collapsed under him. Jacob was virtually lost in the wreckage.

We got him up at last and seated him on a strong bench. When he revived a little I put it to him thus: "Uncle Jacob, are you well this morning? I have never known you to be so affected by three or four drinks as you have been with that bit of Lemonhard." Uncle Jacob looked at me somewhat sheepishly, indeed apologetically, and then the truth struck me—and was subsequently confirmed by Uncle Jacob himself: "When I come out this mornin', about three o'clock, 'twas pretty nippy [there were several icebergs nearby] and I thought about me bottle of rum up in the bureau.* So I went up and got it and took it with me. I shared it with the others and before I knowed it, 'twas gone."

While I know many anecdotes concerning Uncle Jacob I will mention only one other here.

We were going up to Port Hope Simpson, again on a very hot day, and as a concession to the heat Uncle Jacob was persuaded to remove his heavy woollen work gloves. I noticed at this time that his hands had some very strange marks—as if someone had taken a six-inch nail and driven it repeatedly through them. I was curious about this and put the question directly to him. His answer was quite succinct: "That's where the bear got me down and tried to get at me throat."

After a little prodding Jacob overcame his natural modesty and gave me the full story, which was confirmed by all in Port Hope Simpson. He and his buddy had gone rabbit hunting in the woods. Along the way they had encountered a large black bear, and since it appeared to be a bit belligerent, Uncle Jacob shot it—one bullet seemed to do the trick. He then walked up to the carcass. Suddenly it sprang to life, jumped on him, and tried to get at his throat.

---

* A couple of weeks before a St. John's schooner had visited Williams Harbour and, in conformity with established practice, upon departure the skipper left behind a token of esteem in the form of a bottle of dark rum.

But here Jacob's prodigious strength came into play. With only his hands he was able to keep the bear from his throat while lying on his back. His buddy loaded the other gun as fast as he could and tried to find a place to shoot the struggling bear without killing Jacob, but this was more easily said than done. He next tried to stun the bear by hitting it on the tail bone. He only smashed his gun in the process; but this did attract the bear's attention away from Jacob's face and throat momentarily. When the bear next tried to get at a vital spot, Jacob's buddy was able to strike a direct blow with his axe to the bear's skull, splitting it in half.

When Uncle Jacob was finally dragged out from under the bear, he had lost the use of both his hands and feet. Of course, he eventually regained their use, but he carried the scars for the rest of his life.

chapter
13 *White Bay South and Grand Falls*

I remained the member for Labrador for four years and would
have been quite happy to continue to represent one of the two
districts created when the area was divided in 1956. This was in
spite of all the obvious difficulties. For example, proper representation of the district was a continuing problem because of the lack
of roads and the necessity of being away from our home in St.
John's for lengthy periods; and of course, there were also the
added responsibilities of mail, interviews, district functions, representation in the House of Assembly, etc. At the same time, I
had to attend to the supervision of a large government department. My portfolio, Mines and Resources, was easily the largest
department, including as it did agriculture, forestry, water
power, wildlife, Crown lands, mining, geological exploration,
mining inspection, and many other smaller but nonetheless important matters.

Absorbed as I was in this district and departmental work, it came to me almost as a bolt from the blue when in the summer of 1956 Premier Smallwood asked me to vacate my Labrador seat — which everyone was sure would be won by the Liberals by acclamation — for one which was, to me at any rate, a completely unknown factor. My first reaction to the Premier's proposal was negative. I pointed out that I had now invested over four years in Labrador, travelling up and down the coast, meeting just about everyone in the district and working for a variety of improvements. I was quite happy, and was now looking forward to even more achievements since the district had been cut in half as a result of recent legislation. The Premier heard me out; but then he proceeded to advance counterarguments. Among them was the obvious one that even with a split district I would be forced to spend a large portion of my time travelling: each of the two districts would stretch, with indentations, well over 1000 miles. There were other matters, too, that I had to take into consideration. Here are the Premier's approximate words:

> Fred, you and I have to give some thought to the future. If the next election is my last, as it might well be, I would want you to take over. You are too valuable to me and the Party to be so far away from things. You owe it to the province to be more easily accessible.

What was the alternative to Labrador? Another split district, this time the southern half of what was one of the largest districts on the Island: White Bay.

When the first election following Confederation had been held in 1949, White Bay had been a single district stretching from Cape St. John across the Baie Verte Peninsula, around Partridge Point, down to Hampden in the bottom of White Bay, up the west side of White Bay, and then along the whole eastern side of the Great Northern Peninsula to the Strait of Belle Isle. In this huge area there were very few towns of any size apart from St. Anthony, which was the headquarters for the Grenfell Association. The rest of the population was scattered throughout nearly 50 communities, each of which had a population below 1000.

With the exception of St. Anthony, the district lacked the basic facilities of electricity, water, and sewerage. There was only one nursing station in the district, and the one medical doctor served both the community and the logging camps. Also, apart from a few woods roads of little use to the public, the district was without roads of any kind, and for transportation depended almost entirely on service supplied by several small passenger boats and the two coastal ships that travelled from St. John's and Lewisporte. It was this latter situation, above all, that made it a well-nigh impossible district to represent, unless it was divided.

When the first election had been held in 1949, a Liberal candidate, Samuel Drover, had been elected. Drover had been a member of the Ranger police force and had been stationed in what became, after the division, White Bay South, and as a Ranger he had enjoyed a measure of personal support in various places throughout the district. I knew nothing of this until I had started my campaign. But I soon learned.

Of course, the Premier knew what was ahead, but it made no difference to him that White Bay South was one of the two or three districts that I knew little about. His response to this had simply been that this deficiency would be extinguished by one visit through the district.

The election of 1956 was called in September and was held the first week of October. Since there were only two short stretches of road in the district, and apart from this there was nothing but water, my first task in the campaign was to engage a fairly large passenger boat to be not only my mode of transport but my home as well.

I started in the most convenient spot, the bottom of White Bay, which turned out to be the concentration of Drover support. Hampden, Bayside, the Rooms, the Beaches, and several small islands proved to be Drover bastions. Two things were immediately clear to me: if Drover was as strong in other centres as he was in the Hampden area, I was almost certain to lose the district; and if I was going to win I would have to work my head off in other places.

And then I reached Wild Cove, a small village with 72 voters.

As was my custom, I started at one end of the village and visited every home. In general, I found that the residents were inclined to be quiet and reserved and by the end of my village tour I was not sure whether they were going to vote for me or not. However, I had done my best and so I started my way back to the boat which I was using to canvass the district. At that point one of the young men came up to me and enquired whether I had met Uncle Arch. I was not too sure. Then he said, "He's up in the woods," and then, "He's coming now. You'll have to wait for him." And, of course, wait for him I did.

It did not take me long to determine that Arch Small was the patriarch of the village. I had the feeling that it was Uncle Arch who would decide how the vote would go in Wild Cove. After a few more or less cryptic questions and statements on his part, he asked, "Do you know any of the Rowes up around Burnt Bay?" I had to stop for a while, since I wasn't sure about the Burnt Bay bit. I knew that Lewisporte had once been called Big Burnt Bay but there were several places called Burnt Bay.

Rowe: (somewhat hesitantly) Do you mean Lewisporte, Mr. Small?
Uncle Arch: Yes, I think that's what they call it now. There used to be a man Rowe from Burnt Bay who'd come down here for years trading [i.e. trading food and other commodities for fish]. Did you know him?
Rowe: Yes, he was Eli Rowe, my father.
Uncle Arch: (looking at me speculatively) How do you know he's the Rowe I'm talking about?
Rowe: He was the only Rowe in Lewisporte, and he was the only Rowe who traded on the French Shore.*

Uncle Arch looked away in the distance, back over 50 years, as it turned out. Then he started to speak. "One Sunday evening when I was about 20 years old, a schooner came in the harbour and let down anchor. He was going to do some business tomorrow. But I loved baccy and I had no money to buy any. I got in the punt and rowed out to the schooner and climbed on board. There was a man on deck, so I went up to him and asked him if he had a pipeful of baccy to give me. The man said no, he didn't smoke, but the skipper, who was having a snooze down below did, and perhaps he might have one to spare. Not long afterwards another man came up on deck and this turned out to be the skipper. He come up to me and said, 'Was you the man who was looking for some baccy?' I said yes I was, and with that he pulled out a plug of baccy and passed it over. I said, 'No, I can't take that, I haven't got a cent to me name.' And with that the skipper said, 'I likes a smoke myself and I'm not going to see any man stuck for a smoke if I can help it. Here, take the plug and pay me when you sees me again.' I never seen him again, so I never paid him back. But in a couple of weeks I'm going to pay Eli Rowe back for his kindness." And with that Uncle Arch said good-bye.

---

* Wild Cove was on the Treaty Shore of Newfoundland, i.e. that part to which the French fishermen had fishing rights.

I don't know what influence the "plug of baccy" story had, but I do know the records show that every voter in Wild Cove went to the polls on Monday, October 30, 1956, and that all of them voted for Fred Rowe, son of Eli Rowe.

Slowly but surely, I ground down Drover support. Centre after centre, some with sizeable Drover strength, gradually swung around to me. One of the factors I had to overcome was the sympathy vote that some voters made: the task that Drover had taken on in 1949 was an impossible one made all the more difficult for him by the fact that midway through his term he was stricken by tuberculosis and compelled to spend a period in the sanitarium.

When the vote was taken, the only sizeable support for Drover was in the Hampden area, where his popularity with the many young loggers had remained intact. When the vote was counted, I had won by 86 percent, one of the highest in the province. The possible landslide in Drover's favour did not materialize, and the district gave me the same measure of support for the following two elections. (Moreover, when I withdrew, my son Bill ran for two elections in the same district and won by a slightly higher margin than his old man had done—more on that later.)

In retrospect, it was quite clear that Smallwood had some legitimate fears regarding the effect Drover might have had. As my popularity rose, I don't think he actually felt that Drover would win, but given the conditions existing politically at that time a large minority vote for Drover could have had serious repercussions. Hence the Premier's desire for me to run in that district based on his oft-repeated conviction that I was his principal troubleshooter.

Sometimes troubleshooting led me into dealings with interesting people. One of these was K. C. Irving of Irving Oil, just after his company bought out Maritime Mining.

During the 1960s Maritime Mining was an active mining operation under the control of M. J. Boylen, one of Canada's leading mining promoters. The mines concerned were Gull Pond, Tilt Cove, Rambler, and Advocate Mining just outside the town of Baie Verte. As the mines got going, the pressure on local services, especially the schools, became critical almost overnight. The school boards headed by Bishop J. M. O'Neil contacted me, since the mines were all in my district of White Bay South. I was not sure what I could do, since Boylen and his group argued that

Maritime Mining had no legal or moral obligation in the matter. This was probably correct, but I argued in rebuttal that the big industrial groups in Newfoundland, i.e. the paper mills and the big mines, had all accepted some degree of responsibility for the crowded conditions in the schools, and that, invariably, this was in the form of money. When this did not seem to have any effect, I invoked other, more serious arguments, the principal ones being that the mines were making money, that the crowded conditions were the direct result of their operations, and that if the companies continue to shirk their responsibilities, I as the member for the district would not be able to guarantee my good-will.

This implied threat apparently had its effect. Within two or three weeks Boylen contacted me to say that the companies concerned would be willing to give the amount I had asked for, which I believe was $40,000, a good sum in the 1950s. I immediately contacted Bishop O'Neil and his educational colleagues to inform them that on the strength of Boylen's decision — which however had no basis in law — they could go ahead with plans for their two high schools.

It goes without saying that the decision took a great load off my shoulders. But this did not last long. Within a few weeks the announcement was made that Maritime Mining had sold out to a company in which K. C. Irving held the controlling interest. When the school boards requested their money, one of the junior officers of the company informed them that they should go to Mr. Boylen, since it appeared to have been a personal transaction. But Mr. Boylen disclaimed all responsibility and advised the boards to contact Maritime.

Finally I decided to go to K. C. Irving himself and put the whole thing on the table. I told him I knew he had no personal obligation and that if he had to ignore the matter we could not complain. But I also told him about the lack of high school services in White Bay South, where the illiteracy rates were among the highest in Newfoundland. I think I convinced him that, in the long haul, providing high school facilities with all the concomitants would benefit Irving Oil and its many branches in ways not yet known. Irving heard me out passively but politely. When I was finished, he asked, "How much did you say was involved?" "Forty thousand dollars," I replied. He paused for two or three seconds; then he said, "Dr. Rowe, you may inform the Bishop and his friends that a cheque for $40,000 will be in the mail tomorrow." That ended my meeting with one of the richest men in the world.

It is not my intention to give a lengthy recital of the various achievements of the Liberal government. What is worth noting, however, is the revolutionary transformation that took place in White Bay and indeed in most of the outport districts during the two decades from Confederation to the middle 1960s. With respect to White Bay South, here is a synopsis of what was done:

- Every part of the district was linked up by roads with the rest of the district and with the outside world.
- Modern nursing stations were established at La Scie, Jackson's Arm, and Hampden.
- I arranged with my colleague and friend, the distinguished Minister of Health Dr. James McGrath, to go to the British Isles and attempt to recruit doctors for the district. The result was three first-class doctors for Baie Verte, Hampden, and La Scie, which also alleviated the general shortage of medical doctors in Newfoundland.
- Every community in the district received electricity.
- All the larger centres and most of the smaller ones received water and sewerage services.
- The development of the asbestos mine at Baie Verte and the Rambler copper and gold mines a few miles to the east turned Baie Verte into a modern town almost overnight.
- The building and operation of the fishing plant at La Scie and the Tilt Cove copper mine transformed La Scie from a fishing village into a modern industrial town.
- The building of the Callander-Hamilton bridge over the Sops (Main) River linked Sops Arm and Jackson's Arm with the rest of the world.

This list is by no means comprehensive, but it is sufficient to indicate the vast improvement that took place over a few years. For me, personally, it was a source of pride and satisfaction to witness the achievements while in office, and those of my son Bill, who introduced a program of paving that changed for the better large stretches of the Baie Verte Peninsula. However, it should not be assumed that everything done was the result of provincial efforts. The federal authorities also must be given credit for the many public works built during this period.

I have made a few allusions to the dividing of districts. As a rule, such actions were necessary in the interests of fairness and efficiency; in such cases, two factors usually had to be considered, geography and population. But there were other considerations as well, for dividing what had always been a safe Liberal seat often produced the danger that a Tory seat would be created — something that happened on several occasions. The district of St. Barbe, stretching from Bay of Islands to Cooks Harbour, was a good example.

The population of St. Barbe was hardly big enough to warrant division, but from the viewpoint of the second factor, geography, it was a different matter. In the early years after Confederation the area lacked roads, and good harbours were hard to come by. A decision to divide the district into North and South made good sense. Unfortunately, the Premier accepted wrong advice about exactly how to arrange the districts, and the result of the following election was that St. Barbe South went Tory. This particular loss had serious political ramifications in other districts.

Another example, and one that meant more to me personally as it turned out, was the decision to divide what was the largest district on the Island, in both geography and population: Grand Falls. Originally included in that district were Buchans, Windsor, Grand Falls, Bishops Falls, Botwood, and Gander. Clearly, some political surgery was needed. Here, too, the operation was apparently successful, but within a short period both patients died. What had happened was quite simple: the division of this comparatively large district was made by lopping off Botwood, Bishops Falls, and Gander, three of the larger towns in central Newfoundland and all strongly Liberal. Basically what was left was Grand Falls, Windsor, and Buchans. What had been overlooked was that Grand Falls was as big as Windsor and Buchans combined and except for very special circumstances, such as the IWA strike, was Tory. It was only a question of time before it would show its Tory strength and that came in 1962 when the Tory candidate, Ambrose Peddle, defeated the Liberal incumbent, Ray Guy. Here again, the eventual defeat could have been avoided by simply placing Bishops Falls, a strongly Liberal town, with Grand Falls, where it logically belonged.* But the damage was done as far as the next four years or so were concerned and

---

* What may have contributed to the defeat was the fact that Guy, while a member of the House, had been unable to spend much time in his district since, lacking a cabinet post, his income as a backbencher was unlikely to meet his family needs.

the Liberals of Grand Falls (town and district) complained bitterly. It raised Smallwood's hackles that the wealthiest and probably the most progressive district in Newfoundland should be represented by a caustic Tory, and his political acumen told him that as long as Peddle existed he would be a danger.

Here was indeed a problem, but the Liberals of Grand Falls solved it all by themselves, probably with Smallwood's help under the table. A large number of them held a meeting and passed a resolution urging Premier Smallwood to arrange for *me* to be the Liberal candidate in the next election. Smallwood, in accepting the resolution, stated he would do his best with me, but that we were living in a free country.

It was White Bay South over again, with this difference, that Grand Falls, a Tory district, would be a harder nut to crack. Once more I had a hard fight, not with my political enemies so much as with Smallwood. I told him that I had spent ten years in White Bay; that just about all their needs had been met; that my personal standing there had never been higher; and so forth. One circumstance I cited as dangerous was that the people of White Bay South had never given me less than 85 percent in an election, had been highly indignant when they heard of the Grand Falls resolution, and were threatening political rebellion. The matter was further complicated by the fact that large numbers of Tories and nonaligned voters had expressed their pleasure over the request, and that they felt it could only redound to the good of Grand Falls no matter what party was involved.

Once more I was on the horns of a dilemma, as I did not want to see my ten years of grueling work in White Bay South go down the drain. On the other hand, it was clear to me that unless we could find someone with experience and political expertise, Peddle could very well end up in the driver's seat again. There were other factors, too. I felt a kinship with central Newfoundland, and as well many of my Lewisporte relatives had gone to live at Grand Falls. Many nonpartisans were genuinely desirous of seeing me run in Grand Falls.

The one event that probably tipped the scales was that my son, Bill, who was at Oxford as a Rhodes Scholar, indicated his interest in entering politics. His graduation from Oxford coincided with preparations for the provincial election that was to take place in the fall. I was still the member for White Bay South and periodically visited the district. Bill accompanied me on one of these tours and became quite friendly with the voters, especially the young men and women. While we were chatting with a group of residents, someone said to me, "I hear you're going to run in Grand Falls next election—that'll be the end for White Bay." Then another voice spoke up, "We'll let you go if you'll give us Bill." At that the impromptu meeting exploded. Bill did become the member for White Bay South, and represented it for the following two elections.

The election in Grand Falls was fought in a civilized way, as neither Peddle nor I had any desire to resort to roughhouse tactics. Nevertheless, we fought hard and I won with a majority of 709.

My new status as the member for Grand Falls did not affect my way of life too much, because for nearly two years previous to the election, at the request of the Premier and supported by the residents of Grand Falls district, I had served as a sort of liaison between the government and the district; as the member I continued to carry on with the projects that I had been instrumental in activating in the past. For the five years following the election, I worked just as hard and long as for the two years preceding it, to assure the people that they had not made a mistake. The result was a transformation of the district in ways that could be appreciated only by one who had lived in the area for several decades.

The history of my six years as member for Grand Falls provides an excellent example of the uncertainties and vagaries of political life.

I had gone to Grand Falls at the request of the people and in doing so it was obvious that I was giving up a "sure thing" as member for White Bay South. But both Tories and Liberals assured me that once I had established myself, there would be no one who could beat me. On average, I visited the district every three weeks, and once the large public building was completed I arranged for an office with a full-time secretary. As far as Grand Falls district was concerned, the age-old complaint by constituents that they never saw their member was totally invalid. In addition to the official schedules, I received and accepted invitations to hundreds of functions involving schools, clubs, churches, and a host of other groups.

I took scrupulous care to ensure that I visited all the communities regularly, since a favourite device for one's political enemies was to charge the member with spending most of his time in the largest or most attractive centre—in my case, of course, that was

Grand Falls. But with my regular attention, the charge soon became untenable; and if the above measures did not suffice there were always radio and television stations.

It may be of interest to the reader for me to include a typical press release that illustrates what life is like in the average district for the members who keep in touch with all their constituents. On September 14, 1971 I was visiting my district of Grand Falls and my office there issued the following statement:

AGENDA

The member for the Grand Falls district the Honorable Dr. F. W. Rowe arrived in Grand Falls this morning and will be staying in the district until Thursday of this week. Today Dr. Rowe plans to visit Millertown Junction and Gull Bridge Mines. Later today he will be meeting with the Cemetery Committee of Grand Falls and tonight he will be meeting with the Parent-Teachers Association of Badger. Tomorrow night Dr. Rowe will be special guest of the District Liberal Association which will be meeting in the Inland Hotel at Windsor. This meeting will be preceded by a dinner at which Dr. Rowe will be the speaker. Before leaving for St. John's the Minister will be holding a Press Conference at which time he will be dealing with a number of matters of interest to the district.

It has never been my practice to boast about the various achievements in any particular district. Politicians often emphasize the "I" and "we," but in truth individuals and even isolated groups cannot boast very much, since no matter what the project nobody can really claim total responsibility. For example, in the four years or so when I was Minister of Highways we built over half the Trans-Canada Highway, but it could only have been done with the support of my colleagues; and though several of us played a leading role in the development of Memorial University, without the total and dedicated support of Premier Smallwood the university as we know it would never have come into being. But having made this point, it is still a fact that there is usually one person, whether it be the Premier or a particular minister or member, who keeps fighting until a project has been approved or created. It is in this sense that I can claim credit for the following during my six years with Grand Falls:

- Construction of the largest highway garage in Newfoundland
- Purchase and erection of the famous Czechoslovakian pavilion

- Construction at Grand Falls of the second-largest government building in Newfoundland
- Paving or repaving of most of the roads in and around Grand Falls, including the rebuilding and paving of the Buchans and Millertown highways
- Creation of Beothuk Provincial Park and the extension and improvements of Catamaran, Mary March, and Aspen Brook provincial parks
- Assisting over 300 students to get summer work
- Finding permanent jobs for scores of unemployed, many of whom had lost their jobs because of restrictions in the paper mill and in other areas
- Extension and improvement of the central Newfoundland hospital, assistance in building a tourist chalet, and major extension of the Grand Falls Vocational School
- Financial assistance to all the principal hotels in the district
- Guaranteed loans to town councils

The above list, though far from complete, shows that during those years Grand Falls received more help than any other district in the province. This was a matter of dollars and cents and of common sense. And since, as I have indicated, I could hardly be accused of ignoring my constituents, everyone knew that in the next provincial election I was going to "sweep her."

Instead, I was beaten by 386 votes in the most unexpected upset of the election.

Five percent was not much to lose by, but it was enough to puzzle a lot of people after the election was over. Why was I defeated, when I had a record of achievement which, as I was repeatedly told, was the most impressive ever in Newfoundland politics? I queried many of my friends and enemies to try to get at the truth. The answer that I got ad nauseam was that the people of Grand Falls had been determined to "get Smallwood at any cost," and if this meant destroying Fred Rowe politically — well, it was too bad. They regretted to see me go, but if my defeat was a prerequisite to Smallwood's, then so be it.

I have always considered this explanation too simplistic and unfair to the hundreds who voted for me, in many cases knowing I would be defeated. It puts all the blame on all the anti-Smallwood voters, when in reality the blame should be distributed all over, as the actual vote was. Another factor which, in retrospect, should have been apparent to the Liberals and to the undecided was complacency. To put it another way, too many people, many of them Liberal, felt that Rowe couldn't be defeated, and that, this being so, a vote against that so-and-so Smallwood wouldn't hurt.

Another factor that probably did as much as anything to turn voters against the Liberal Party was the sense of insecurity and outright fear that prevailed in the latter half of 1970 and still more strongly in 1971. In the winter of 1971, for example, the Buchans mine, the largest and most prosperous on the Island of Newfoundland, went on strike and remained on strike until past the 1971 election. In that year, too, the great Grand Falls paper mill closed down for three periods of three weeks each, thus not only affecting the pockets of the workers but giving the undecided voters, who normally decide which way the district will go, a good opportunity to try out the other party. With help from the NDP, the PCs grasped the opportunity to oust the Liberals.

chapter
14 *The Vagaries of Politics*

On July 8, 1968 Premier Smallwood announced that he would be retiring from active politics and therefore would not be running in the next provincial election. Many people were astonished to hear this, since it had long been a tenet of political faith that like a lot of other famous political figures Smallwood would remain in politics until he had to be carried out. I was among the skeptical, although Smallwood assured me repeatedly that he was indeed finished. He also expressed to me more and more a fear that if none of the old-time Liberals entered the picture the leadership would go to John Crosbie by default, and this was a clear hint he wanted me to run.

I hesitated to enter the race. Crosbie was actively recruiting potential delegates, and there was a chance that come September, when the leadership convention was due to start, I would find myself with a minority. It was true that if Smallwood supported me, as he had publicly stated he would, Crosbie would most likely end up with about only one-third of the votes. But would Smallwood support me or decide to run despite his assurances? There was yet another factor that had to be considered. Smallwood was still healthy, but he was now 70 and had worked hard; sooner or later his heart or vascular system would be protesting. Much could happen in the 12 months before the convention.

I finally arrived at a compromise decision. In January 1969 I announced that I would be running for the leadership of the Liberal Party in the convention to be held in the fall of that year, but — and this was a very big "but" — that if Premier Smallwood decided to run again I would withdraw from the race and support him.

Among those indicating their pleasure over my decision, none showed greater enthusiasm than Smallwood. In addition to making a number of oral statements about his pleasure and support, Smallwood wrote to me semi-formally on January 10; his opening paragraph was:

> It has been well understood between us for a dozen years or more that you would be offering yourself as a candidate for the leadership of the Liberal Party when I step aside as a leader, and you now assure me that it is your firm intention to do so in the immediate future. I am deeply pleased over your decision and I know that your announcement will be received warmly by a great many Liberals throughout our Province. . . .

Among other statements made by Smallwood during this critical period was the following:

> I am deeply pleased with Dr. Rowe's decision to offer himself for the leadership of the Liberal Party. He is the most experienced Cabinet Minister there has ever been in Newfoundland. He has been head of more different departments of government than any man before him. . . . It was at my invitation that Dr. Rowe occupied these various positions. My purpose in having him do so was to enable him . . . to acquire an ever broader experience in the business of running a government.

Having made the decision to run, my next step was to set up an organization. I invited my son Fred, then an assistant professor at Memorial University, to become my manager. Offices were established in the Avalon Mall with two university students employed to assist us. Among those indicating their intention to support me were all the delegates in Grand Falls and the majority of delegates in Lewisporte, Gander, White Bay, Labrador, and other outport districts.

For the next five months, slow but steady progress was made in my campaign. In fact, all indications were that, given funds roughly equal to Crosbie's resources, and with Smallwood's support, I would win by a substantial majority.

We continued to make progress through winter and spring, and then in July, with the convention called for September, Smallwood announced that he was re-entering the race.

On hearing of Smallwood's decision, I kept my pledge made in January and announced that I would support his leadership. Many of my friends urged me to continue in the race, but in doing so they ignored an important point. Assuming I would carry a sizeable personal vote, there was the danger (from a Liberal standpoint) that I would siphon off enough votes from Smallwood to make it difficult for him to hold onto a respectable majority, and without a majority Smallwood would have had to carry on under very difficult conditions.

As it turned out, even with me no longer in the running, the 1969 convention was one of the most vicious in Newfoundland history, and while Smallwood won by a good majority, the Party was split for years to come. That convention—costing probably a million or more dollars and virtually bankrupting the Liberal Party—achieved nothing, but simply maintained the status quo, while driving Crosbie and his people into the Tory camp. It also paved the way for the debacle of the October 1971 election, when the Liberals were brought low.*

It is part of the mythology of Newfoundland politics—indeed, of democratic politics everywhere—that the party in power is usually elected by a solid majority of the electorate, but from the day of the election onward there is a steady decline that eventually leads to the demise of the party. Smallwood and the experience of the Liberal Party are frequently invoked as examples. The truth is that this is too neat an explanation, that rarely is there a graph starting at the top and gradually but inevitably projecting to the bottom; it does not withstand scrutiny in the light of cold fact.†

---

* Had the Liberals been able to close ranks for the next election, held in March 1972 by order of the Lieutenant Governor, it is quite possible that they could have prevented the even greater disaster that followed. But they didn't, and that is another story waiting to be told.

† Alberta provided the supreme example when the Social Credit Party, after 25 years in power, suddenly won every seat.

Through the more than 22 years that Smallwood was in power, there was not a steady decline in the fortunes of the Liberal Party; in fact, there were periods when there was no decline. Here are a few statistics to help throw light on this matter.

SEATS HELD BY PROVINCIAL PARTIES IN NEWFOUNDLAND

YEAR	LIBERAL	PC	UN*	INDE-PENDENT
1949	22	5		1
1951	23	5		
1956	32	4		
1959	31	3	2	
1962	34	7		1
1966	39	3		

* A splinter group from the PCs known as the United Newfoundland Party.

It is clear that as far as representation in the House of Assembly was concerned, there was some fluctuation, but not much. The only significant decline occurred between 1959 and 1962: in the 1962 election the PCs garnered 7 members and 1 independent emerged, making the opposition 8. But between 1962 and 1966 massive positive changes occurred, resulting in the province's becoming as strongly Liberal as it had ever been, the Liberals capturing 39 seats and the PCs only 3. This is attributable to the fact that in education, roads, bridges, paving, parks, schools, tourism, mighty changes were taking place under the Liberals.

But then came October 1971, when the Liberals were brought low. Why? One can only guess. My own feeling — after the frustration of weeks and months of having my advice repeatedly dismissed or ignored — is that two major factors were responsible: (1) the unnecessary and ill-advised tampering with the district partitioning and in selection of candidates;* (2) the antagonizing,

---

* As an example of the latter, no one consulted me about replacing Harold Starkes, who had been elected several times in Lewisporte by large majorities, by a young man belonging to the Pentecostal church on the grounds that 30 percent of Lewisporte had that religious affiliation. Apparently it was not known that most of the other 70 percent were United Church. The new candidate was not elected.

again unnecessarily, of large and influential groups, e.g. teachers, university students, nurses, and policemen, to the point where they did not hesitate to campaign against the Liberals. There were other factors, of course, not the least of which being the failure to appreciate the absolute necessity of calling the election before the teachers and university were able to meet and consolidate their forces—i.e. at least by the first week of September. The story of this unexplicable decision has been dealt with elsewhere. Suffice it to say that, in my opinion, in 1971 the Liberal Party was defeated by the Liberal Party.

As far as I know, the nine portfolios that I held during the 20 years I was in provincial politics constitutes something of a record. Education and Finance were each my portfolios on two occasions (widely separated). Several times I carried two portfolios for lengthy periods; for example, I once handled both Finance and Labrador Affairs.

I have frequently been asked, "What portfolio did you find most difficult? Most rewarding? Most challenging?" Some departments of government were more difficult than others if for no other reason than the sheer volume of work; the Department of Mines and Resources comes to mind. It comprised the following: agriculture, forestry, Crown lands, wildlife, geology, mining, water and water power, and several miscellaneous divisions. Any one of the above would normally be sufficient to warrant a small- or medium-sized department of its own. In my opinion, Mines and Resources was simply too big to be handled properly. For example, Crown land grants, of which there would be hundreds in the course of a year, had to be examined and signed by the minister. This meant that I, as Minister, had work piling up on my desk from the two deputy ministers, the directors, and other senior officials, and the only way I could handle it was by working on my weekends. By comparison with Mines and Resources, the Department of Finance, though extremely important, was not very demanding.

The Department of Education required interminable meetings and conferences, endless school functions all over the province, and all the while looking after the routine affairs of the department and attending Cabinet meetings—which, though a common responsibility, pressed most heavily on the ministers of the larger departments.

Perhaps the simplest way to answer the question would be to refer to the old cliché that a person can be as busy as he wants to be — and I suppose, by inference, as lazy as he wishes. For my part, I found enough work in my departments to keep me busy. On occasion, I resented it a little that I always seemed to have heavy departments; but that feeling was only temporary. Usually I enjoyed the work no matter what the department.

PART 4

SENATOR ROWE 1972–1987

chapter

15 *The Senate*

With the defeat of the Liberal Party in 1971, the question that immediately arose was what to do with the dead bodies, especially the older ones. I had been Minister of Finance, President of the Council, and Deputy Premier when the cataclysm struck. To the best of my knowledge, nothing whatsoever had been done in anticipation of the possibility of a political disaster, and for a certainty I had done nothing for myself.

The first person in a responsible position to approach me was Smallwood. I knew, as most of our party knew, that he was being besieged by Liberals (and others, too, I would imagine) regarding the senatorial seat left vacant earlier that year by Malcolm Hollett. But without beating around the bush, Smallwood said, "Fred, if you want the Hollett seat it's yours for the asking." Since, technically, the appointment of a senator is in the Prime Minister's hands, and since the Prime Minister would undoubtedly consult with the Liberal representative in the Cabinet, I felt sure Smallwood had paved the way before making such an unequivocal offer to me.

Perhaps, at this juncture, I should go back a bit. Between the election and the filling of the Senate seat there was a lapse of about six weeks during which my family and friends made their feelings known to me without any hesitation: they were unanimous in urging me to go into the Senate. But I had some reservations. I was barely 59 years old, and there was nothing to say that I was finished with active politics (this time in a Liberal district but there were other considerations). Also, with three university degrees, including a doctorate, and with vast experience in every aspect of education, I did not envision myself thumping the sidewalks very long with my hand out begging for a job either in the public or the private sector. Finally, when Smallwood came to discuss the Senate with me he confirmed something he had spoken to me about earlier, namely that if I did not want to go into the Senate there was a federal position waiting for me with a ten-year contract and a salary somewhat larger than what the Senate was then offering; the Prime Minister confirmed this. Thus, I was surrounded by a plethora of riches, if job opportunities meant anything.

Yet curiously, though these opportunities were a factor, there was only one matter that prevented me from accepting the Senate seat right from the start: I was under the totally erroneous impression that an appointment to the Senate meant living in Ottawa, and this my wife was not prepared to accept unless it became an issue of bread and butter. She had been living in St. John's for nearly 30 years, had many friends there, was a topnotch bridge player and bowler, and, most important of all, wanted to be near her grandchildren; this whole pattern would be disturbed if we went to live in Ottawa.

It was one of my sons who set me straight. One day he said to me, "Dad, where did you get this idea that being a senator means having to live in Ottawa all the time?" I had to confess I had no authority for it; I had simply taken it for granted. (In retrospect, I probably got the notion from the Newfoundland senators, most of whom had lived there.) The question got me asking around, and to my infinite surprise I found that not only did the central Canada appointees live in Toronto or Montreal or wherever, but the great majority of westerners also lived at home and most of them were farther from Ottawa than the Newfoundland senators were. Moreover, senators could go to their home town on weekends or whenever they wished. Some of those who did so had homes or apartments in Ottawa; others — the majority, of whom I became one—stayed at one of the hotels (usually the Château Laurier) and went home on Thursday evenings unless there was special business that warranted the Senate's remaining open.

Possessed of this information I let it be known to Premier Smallwood that I would accept a senatorship. Less than a week later, early on a Sunday morning, I received a call from Prime Minister Trudeau advising me that if I was willing he would recommend me for appointment, and I accepted immediately. I should say here that Trudeau, whom I had met a number of times before he became prime minister and with whom I had spent part of a day at Smallwood's home at Roache's Line, appeared pleased with the transaction. Also, Trudeau did not mention Donald Jamieson but there was no doubt in my mind that he had cleared the decision with Don. Thus, I had the pleasure of feeling that all three of the key men involved were pleased with my appointment.

So, on December 9, 1971 I became member of the Senate of Canada. In my first speech to the Senate, on March 1, 1972, I referred to the moral and practical necessity of making Canada bilingual; the approaching rebellion among the youth not just of Canada but in most parts of the democratic world; the need to differentiate between marijuana and heroin and other hard drugs; a radical revision of the Criminal Code and the penal system; the abolition of strikes as an instrument of economic policy; and the abuses and antisocial behaviour of big business, particularly the tobacco, automobile, and legitimate drug interests. I also addressed the simple arithmetical fact that tobacco and alcohol were the two most serious problems in the world; and urged that the pattern established by the Senate in recent years of initiating investigations into poverty, scientific developments, the mass media, etc. be broadened and intensified, since no other body in Canada was in so favourable a position to carry out such enquiries.

Had someone told me, when I first entered the Senate, that I knew practically nothing about it and its functions, I would have felt most indignant; yet it would have been true. For example, it was a revelation to me that the Senate does more work through its standing, special, and joint committees than in the full session.

The committee system is simplicity itself. When a new parliament is formed, a Committee of Selection that reports to the full Senate is set up for the purpose of manning the standing, special, and joint committees. Normally, though there are bound to be difficulties in meeting all wishes, persons wanting to be on a particular committee can be fitted in.

The standing committees, as the name implies, are regular committees — whose work, however, ceases with the prorogation of a parliament. Legislation coming from the Commons or to the Senate itself is routinely referred to the appropriate standing committee. In earlier days, this procedure occasioned little turbulence; not so today, as the debates on the Meech Lake and the pharmaceutical legislation have shown.

If a report of any committee is accepted by the Senate, the committee meets and selects a chairman and a vice-chairman. In general, the chairman is some member with a good deal of experience and expertise in the field covered by the committee. For years, one of the best-known committees was that of Banking, Trade, and Commerce, and its chairman was Senator Salter Hayden of the great law firm of McCarthy and McCarthy. Though Senator Hayden remained in that post until he was well into his eighties, all his faculties stayed crystal-clear. And it is no accident that the present chairman, Senator Ian Sinclair, is a man who has had enormous experience in the world of business and commerce.

There are few "average" members in the Senate. As would be expected in an institution that has over 100 members, many senators have been in positions of trust and responsibility prior to their appointment. A few years ago, no fewer than five former provincial premiers were serving in the Senate. Other selections are made from time to time, not of tired and worn-out political hacks, as some columnists have described them, but of vigorous and alert men and women from every walk of life, many of them middle-aged or younger. For example, some of Canada's outstanding lawyers have been and are active there. Royce Frith, deputy leader of the opposition in the Senate, is an excellent example, as are Senators Joan Neiman, Jacques Flynn, Gerry Graftstein, Daniel Lang, and at least 20 others.

The Senate of Canada has been discussed, criticized, blasphemed, and even praised so much in recent years that it seems impossible to find anything new or refreshing to say about it. When I became a member the main topic of conversation was reform of the Senate. When I left in September 1987 the main topic of conversation was reform of the Senate. In between, there had been endless discussions and reports, but nothing ever came of them.

I myself had made a number of suggestions. I knew next to nothing about the Senate, but in one sense I welcomed this since it allowed me to approach the problem without preconceived notions. After meeting with some people regarded as experts on the matter and reading whatever was then available, I wrote a couple of newspaper articles wherein I dealt with a few matters usually misunderstood and recommended a number of changes. Though none of it was earthshaking, most of those who read the articles were kind enough to express approval. But to this day nothing was really done, even though my recommendations could have been carried out without having to mutilate the constitution.

What was true on a small scale was true on a larger scale with the special committees, but here too nothing was done. What, for example, was there to prevent the western provinces from having stronger Senate representation? I cannot help but feel that if the Senate had been more determined and had applied more pressure, the government and members of the House of Commons would have been more responsive. But that chance is probably no longer going to be available without constitutional upheavals of a serious nature.

In September of my first full year as a senator, I addressed the Inter-Parliamentary Union in Rome, Italy on the subject of drugs. What I said in Rome I have stressed and repeated in one way or another on a number of occasions in the Senate. Nothing that I have observed in those years has changed my basic beliefs, and still the danger looms, but it is now rapidly developing into a worldwide threat. With this in mind, I would like to summarize here the speech I made on that occasion.

There is no way to confine the drug problems to one city or country and there is no reason why the so-called soft drugs need to be equated with the hard ones. The whole problem is complicated by the almost total inconsistency in the application of punitive measures from city to city and country to country. These measures may extend from a slap on the wrist to the death penalty. No one can justify these horrifying attitudes, so often apparent, and yet ignore our attitude toward the two most serious problems of all, alcohol and tobacco.

While no one would argue that all tobacco and alcohol addicts should be incarcerated, society is entitled to know why there is so much discrimination with respect to, say, marijuana users. Then, too, little recognition is accorded to the fact that teenagers and older people who are subjected to a jail experience for six or twelve months or longer are almost guaranteed to come out of jail poisoned against society and certainly more skillful lawbreakers than they were when they went in.

No one today believes that marijuana is a harmless drug, or that it is nonaddictive. But in the United States and Canada alone there are millions who have used marijuana and other soft drugs and have certainly suffered no more harm in the long run than have excessive tobacco users. Because so many of the off-shoots of excessive smoking are insidiously hidden, it is difficult for scientists to assess its true dimensions insofar as damage to the body system is considered. What is almost certain is that the damage is enormous. Our approach to the problem, however, should be tempered by our recognition of what happened 60-odd years ago when the United States decided to approach the issue of alcohol on an emotional and irrational basis. The result was to change what had hitherto been a relatively law-abiding country into a gangster- and crime-ridden society which to this day has not been able—in spite of the repeal of Prohibition—to cope with the criminal structure which, deprived of its basic commodity, turned to other drugs and other criminal activities.

As far as dangerous drugs are concerned, we may soon be reaching the point of no return—the point at which disease becomes irreversible and uncontrollable. To cope with that possibility, which becomes more menacing every day, intelligent action on a collective basis is absolutely imperative.

16 *Friends from the Senate*

During my 16 or so years in the Senate, I have had interesting conversations and experiences with my fellow members, but the constraints of space mean that many stories will have to remain in my memory. My selection is purely personal, nor is there any attempt at priority. Others who could well have been included here are Henry Hicks, Lorne Bonnell, Harper Prowse, and John M. Macdonald. The following anecdotes should be understood as a cross-section of the senatorial community.

Like many other Canadians, I had heard and read about Hazen Argue, but I don't think I had met him before I became a senator. In one particular afternoon session I got into an argument with Senators Joe Sullivan and Allister Grosart, probably about marijuana or other drugs. Without warning, Hazen entered the fray and attacked Sullivan and Grosart right and left. After the Senate closed I went to his desk and the conversation went something like this:

Rowe: Hazen, I didn't know you felt so strongly about these matters.
Hazen: Oh, I don't feel so strongly at all. In fact I have no strong views whatever.
Rowe: Well, in that case, why did you enter the debate?
Hazen: I didn't like the way Sullivan and Grosart jumped on you. You're new here and I thought I should lend you a hand when things got rough. But you handled yourself all right anyway.

Needless to say, I have been an admirer of Hazen ever since.

Sidney L. Buckwold ("Sid") was one of a group summoned to the Senate in the fall of 1971. He had been mayor of Saskatoon and president of the Canadian Federation of Municipalities, to mention only two of his accomplishments. To these should be added his ever-present sense of humour and vast repertoire of jokes.

This story concerns Sid's lifelong friend John Diefenbaker. Since they were on opposite sides politically, both Sid and the Chief were wise enough to recognize that neither could afford to antagonize the other. However, from time to time one would try to outflank the other.

As all the world knows, Diefenbaker made meticulous plans for his own funeral, including selection of his honorary pallbearers. Among those chosen was Senator Buckwold, but the Chief had made a bit of a faux pas in that he had included Sid's name without his permission. This had to be rectified. Accordingly, when a week or so later as the Chief was returning from the main dining room where he always had his meals, he encountered Sid on his way to dinner, he stopped and the following dialogue took place:

Diefenbaker: Ah, Sidney. I've been hoping to see you on a little matter.
Buckwold: Yes, Mr. Diefenbaker, can I be of service in any way?
Diefenbaker: That remains to be seen. I've been making some plans for my demise which [with a twinkle] no doubt will come some time.
Buckwold: Looking as healthy as you do, that matter is a long way off, I'm sure.
Diefenbaker: Well, we'll see.* Now to business. I have drawn up a list of my friends of all political tenets to be honorary pallbearers and I have included you among them. Would you be willing to serve?
Buckwold: Nothing would give me greater pleasure.

---

* He died about a year later.

Pause. Mr. Diefenbaker looked at Sid severely. Realizing his unfortunate choice of words, Sid started to turn red. Then came the clincher from the Chief: "I thought so."

Of all of the members still serving in the Senate, probably no one has had such a varied career as David Croll, now the senior member by virtue of senatorial appointment. To begin with, Senator Croll was born in Moscow; and though he left when he was only five years old and there is no sign whatever of any language other than English, I suspect he could summon others if required.

At 25 he was a lawyer, and at the age of 30 he was mayor of Windsor. From 1934 to 1944, he was a member of the Ontario legislature, serving as Minister of Public Welfare, Municipal Affairs, and Labour over that period. From 1939 to 1945 he was on active service, rising from the rank of private to that of colonel. Finally, in 1955 he was summoned to the Senate and has been there ever since.

Croll has the unique distinction of being both the first Jewish cabinet minister and the first Jewish senator in Canada. When a statement of that kind is made today people are inclined to raise their eyebrows: "So what? Jews are leaders in every walk of life today. What's strange about that?" But when David Croll came to Canada in the year 1905 Jews were not prominent. How the situation has changed! Half the time now we don't know what racial or religious group a mayor or cabinet minister may belong to. And we don't care.

The Senate arrangement is the same as that of the House of Commons in that each unit has two seats. I was in the Senate for nearly 16 years and in that time I sat in five different seats, which gave me different seatmates. (I never knew how I obtained a particular seat, or who was responsible for the allocation. Presumably the whips and the Speaker's office or the Black Rod played some part.) On my second transfer I found that my new seatmate was Margaret Norrie, whom I had never met before. It was a happy arrangement, for Margaret was one of nature's kindliest and gentlest creatures—except when she saw a piece of injustice or inequity.

Margaret Norrie was not one to boast of family connections, but she grew up in the home of a university president, Dr. George Truman, and is one of the New Brunswick Fawcetts.

This fascinating woman was left a widow with several children and a farm and other enterprises to manage, which she did and still raised a family who adored her. She has left us now, but my wife and I loved her as one of our own, and we both thank whoever gave me that seat next to Margaret. It was never dull.

I have always been proud of the fact that when I was summoned to the Senate the first native Indian was summoned also. We soon became friends and have remained so ever since. We had never met before our appointments, but actually, without realizing it, we had had dealings with each other over several years.

When in the 1950s the Newfoundland government decided to take advantage of Newfoundland's unique opportunities to breed and raise mink, we decided that the best way to approach the matter would be to enlist the help of people already in the business. We could best do that by encouraging the west-coast mink raisers to come to Newfoundland, where, among other things, cheap whale meat was abundantly available for a food supply.

I was Minister of Mines and Resources and the mink program came under that department. Smallwood was, of course, the prime mover, and with his infectious enthusiasm he soon had a good proportion of the western Canadian mink interests clamouring to be included in the program. Everything went well for several years and then — disaster. Some form of disease struck the mink, destroying their ability to breed; as the older mink died there were no young to replace them. Every attempt to cope with the problem failed. The great mink industry that had promised to be one of the world's greatest simply fizzled out — and one of those ruined that I heard of was a Guy Williams.

It was probably because Guy never visited the province that I did not find out until a year or more after our appointments that the Guy Williams of mink fame was the Guy Williams of the Senate of Canada. The dénouement went something like this:

Rowe: Guy, there used to be a Guy Williams involved in the Newfoundland mink industry. Was he related to you?
Williams: (after scrutinizing my face) Related? I was the poor sucker who lost over half a million dollars on the damn stuff. Was I related!

Guy had been a professional heavyweight wrestler and weighed over 300 pounds, so before I pursued the next question I looked around for the quickest way to escape in case I had to run.

Rowe: Did you know any of the Newfoundland people you had dealings with?

Williams: Oh yes, there was a guy Rowe who headed up the program under Smallwood. [Then his jaw dropped as the dawn of knowledge came.] Yes. He was Fred Rowe and *you're* the son of a gun.

Rowe: (disappearing through the door) I'll see you later, Guy.

I did not see Guy for several days, but when I did he greeted me with gales of laughter, and from that time on whenever we were at a function, Guy would relate how "my best friend cleaned me out of a half-million dollars."

I have used the expression "one of nature's gentlemen" somewhere, but it is worth repeating to describe Guy Williams. Honesty, dignity, and integrity are some of the words that come to mind whenever I think of him. He did not know how to be mean or unfair or unreasonable. I was pleased when he and I became senators together and I was sorry when he left.

When I entered the Senate in 1971, one of the most prominent members on the opposition or Tory side was Allister Grosart. I had met him only once before, when by chance I was in Smallwood's office as Grosart paid him a complimentary visit. I found him to be somewhat condescending, the result perhaps of the fact that the Conservative Party under Diefenbaker was in a period of ascendency. In any case, with Smallwood present other Liberals did not do much talking.

This was an unpropitious beginning, and when I next met Grosart, this time in the Senate of Canada, matters did not seem to improve: when I got up to speak he would listen for two or three minutes, and then with an aside to one of his colleagues he would walk out of the chamber. I assumed from this action that the situation had reached the point where he simply disliked me and had no desire to hear anything I might try to say. Well, since Grosart had no desire to hear me out, I saw no great reason to extend the usual courtesies. As far as I was concerned, I had leaned over backwards on several occasions, only to have this man turn his back on me.

This rather childish state of affairs continued for several years. Eventually, however, I felt that I should make greater efforts to rationalize the matter, and I discovered some facts that threw light on Grosart's behaviour. Before coming to the Senate, I had been a member of the Newfoundland legislature for 20 years, and there the loudspeaker system was not as powerful as I later found the Senate system to be. Thinking about it, I hit on the idea that from long practice I, and probably several other Newfoundlanders, tended to speak louder and to stand closer to the microphone than necessary in the Senate chamber. There was another factor as well. For some reason unknown to me, the two personal sound systems used to get crossed in some way. Whatever the reason or combination of reasons, poor Grosart was on the receiving end of continual blasting from Rowe. Presumably, after standing the ordeal for three or four minutes, he had to leave in order to preserve his sanity.

Once I had worked out the mechanics of the problem, it was simple for me to move back a couple of feet from my microphone or to turn it off altogether. Grosart and I never did become bosom friends, but at least we learned to tolerate each other. His death was a loss to Canada.

Norman Paterson had to be one of the most distinctive members of the Senate by any account. Born in central Canada (Manitoba) hundreds of miles from contact with the ocean, he became one of Canada's leading ship owners and grain merchants. His seat was directly across the chamber from mine, and in my early days in the Senate we chitchatted quite often. (As the years slipped by, however, he seemed to withdraw more. Most of his friends attributed this to his very old age, which was made more evident by the walking stick which he invariably carried in his later years.)

I shall never forget the explanation he gave me of how he had come to be so closely associated with the sea — one which, if taken at face value, must be regarded as one of the most interesting to be found in the annals of commercial history. Though Senator Paterson was an extremely modest man, he was always ready to express his views from his Senate seat. And there was one matter on which he seemed to regard himself as an authority: ships and shipwrecks. I well remember his comments to me at the time when a very large cargo ship had been lost with all hands on one of the Great Lakes. I ventured to query him about the accident, and he did not hesitate to cite ineptitude on the part of some of the crew and maintain that the boat should not have gone down. I believe it was on that occasion that I said to him, "Senator Paterson, I find it a little strange that one born and raised, as you were, in Portage la Prairie, several hundred miles from salt water, should end up as one of the leading ship owners in the world. There must be some explanation." "Yes, there is," he replied. "Some years ago I bought all the grains I could get hold of, only to find that my competitors had bought or leased all the ships in an attempt to ruin me. I said to myself, 'I cannot let this happen again.' So I went out and founded my own shipping line." The great shipping line of N. M. Paterson was the result.

PART 5 MEMORABILIA

17 *Escapades of Youth*

*I*n the early 1920s the Grenfell Association had a magnificent yacht, *Strathcona II*. It was given to Grenfell by Lord Strathcona, who, having worked in several Labrador posts as an official of the Hudson's Bay Company, had a more than passing interest in Grenfell's work. This yacht was so beautiful and so spic-and-span that it was the talk of Newfoundland, and to me, who had had Grenfell's sainthood drilled into my ears for several years, the very name of this ship evoked images that could hardly be described.

One afternoon in early summer when I was ten or eleven, I happened to look toward the public wharf, about a half-mile as the crow flew, and there to my complete astonishment floated the most beautiful boat I had ever seen. It was getting too near suppertime to do anything about this phenomenon, but I went into the house and cajoled my mother to give me my meal a bit earlier than usual. Then I left the house as quietly and unobstrusively as possible, and once out of sight of it probably set a new record for the half-mile.

When I reached the massive wharf there was only one person to be seen. My object now was to get on board this nautical vision and so I chatted nonchalantly with the man there, taking care not to arouse his suspicions. In the meantime I elicited from him the information that the ship had come to Lewisporte to connect with the Grenfell volunteers — usually medical students from American universities — who were due in Lewisporte on the 1 a.m. train. The only person then on the ship, I was told, was the Doctor himself.

My informant's attention was soon diverted elsewhere, giving me a chance to slip on board this beautiful boat with its brass and mahogany.* Once on board I walked along the gangway, feasting my eyes on a multitude of wonders. Soon I came to a passageway which was somewhat dark and decided to go in. I froze, however, when I saw at the end of the passageway a grey-haired man sitting at a desk reading a book. I remember noticing that the passageway was lit at the end by a candle or lamp and the thought flashed across my mind that this might be a method of conserving electricity, but any reflections on these or other matters were cut short when the Doctor turned and sprang to his feet, demanding, "What are you doing on this boat? Who told you to come on board?"

Aware of the falseness of my position, the only response I could manage was to gulp repeatedly, so Grenfell ordered, "Get ashore immediately and don't ever come on board again." I was already backing out, and my only reply was to gulp once more.

When I reached the pier, I probably broke more records in getting ashore. I have wondered many times why Grenfell was so untypically harsh on that occasion.

Gus Boone and I had a number of things in common: we were the same age, we lived near each other, and we loved adventure. That meant we were bound to get into trouble together. Gus's father, an engineer on the branch railway, was the highest-paid man in Lewisporte; in busy times he would get as much as $200 a month; and since there was only one other child in the family, the

---

* This was no great achievement for a Lewisporte boy, since with coastal steamers almost continually coming and going and with the countless number of boats of all sizes using the harbour, most of us considered ourselves authorities on these matters.

father could be generous almost beyond belief. This trait manifested itself in a variety of ways, the most spectacular of which was
his one day giving Gus a bicycle. It was the first one ever seen in
Lewisporte, and overnight Gus became the most popular member
of our group. We flattered, threatened, cajoled—anything to be
able to ride the bicycle. Not too long after this, life became still
more complicated when Gus's father acquired a small but beautiful motorboat in which he installed a three-horsepower Acadia
marine engine.

One day Gus suggested that instead of going to school, we
should "mooch," i.e. play hooky. Ordinarily, I was able to tolerate a reasonable amount of school incarceration. But since it was
a June afternoon under a cloudless sky, I succumbed to Gus's
blandishments. Unfortunately we would have to forget about
using either the bike or the boat, because it would be impossible
to go undetected on the mirror-like harbour or on the limited
road system, and news of our defection would spread like wildfire
—fanned most of all by our schoolmates, who, since they could
not share in the deviltry, would make sure they spoiled our fun.

Clearly, any venture would have to be kept absolutely private,
a practice that Gus had been called on to observe more than
once. I don't know which one of us thought of the plan first, but
we were in complete agreement. The railway ran on behind the
community, and once we were back of our house there was
nothing to impede us. We would get our trout poles and walk up
the railway just over a mile to Big Brook.*

The plan worked perfectly. When we reached the Brook area
we left the railway track and walked the short stretch to where the
Lewisporte road and the Brook intersected. There, right under
the bridge, was the "pool of pools." We knew there were trout
aplenty in the Brook and we made ready accordingly, but little
did we suspect, as we dropped hook, line, and worm into the
water, that not one but two beautiful young salmon were waiting.
Within seconds, they were lying on the bank.

It was the first salmon that we 12-year-olds had ever caught
and we thirsted to return to our buddies who had not been able to
share our adventure and glamour. And so we immediately set off
for home, each of us with his salmon dangling proudly from a

---

* So named because it was the bigger of the two brooks flowing into Lewisporte
  Harbour.

bamboo pole. As we reached the built-up area, however, for me one nasty question kept obtruding: How could I explain to my parents the how, when, and where of this beautiful catch? Gus could offer no help, and of course he had the same problem.

By the time we arrived at my house there was only one heart-breaking opportunity left to conceal our guilt. A few hundred feet to the west of the house was a very thick grove of spruce and fir. The pole I did not worry about, for almost daily we could be seen fishing from one of the wharves; but no one would believe we got our salmon that way, so into the woods, as far as I could throw, went the salmon, with Gus following suit.

To add insult to injury, Gus and I could not even boast about our catch, since if the story reached our parents' ears, the inevitable would happen.

There were other incidents and episodes involving Gus and me. Because Mr. Boone was a senior operating officer of the Lewisporte railway, his sons, Gus and Ches, carried a lot of weight on the premises. The roundhouse, for example, was a place of utter fascination, especially when Gus, taking advantage of the brief absence of the engineering crew, learned the mastery of those mighty engines. What was a complete mystery to me became routine to Gus, who was never hesitant about providing the rest of us with information on how to use brakes, lever, and throttle. To the best of my knowledge, only once did Gus underestimate the forces he was able to control; the result was a mysterious injury to the end of the roundhouse.

Curiously enough, Gus and I never became lasting friends, but at no time did we ever have a serious falling-out. And on one occasion he had more than a passing gratitude for my swimming proficiency when he became tangled in water lilies or kelp of some kind, and without my help he would probably have finished his career right then and there.

Gus was able to reciprocate a few years later. I had long har-boured a desire to do what no one had done so far: swim across Lewisporte Bay. On a lovely summer evening when everything was propitious, i.e. when the water was warm and there was no wind, I decided to give it a try. But I needed a boat and an atten-dant, since being a half-mile away from shore could involve dangerous problems. I was familiar with Lewisporte waters and knew there were cold currents, but in the back of my mind were other possibilities: predatory fish, swordfish, dogfish (small and

vicious sharks), and whales of various kinds. Most of these creatures were probably harmless to human beings, but one could
never be sure. A rowboat could keep pace with me, and in case of
emergency I could be helped into the boat. In other words, I
needed Gus, and Gus I got, just as soon as he heard about my
plan.

During the crossing only one untoward incident occurred. I
was using the side stroke to keep my vision clear, and I pushed my
arm into the midst of one of those huge blood-red jellyfish. I
almost jumped out of the water. But I got away from those ten-
tacles without difficulty and continued until my feet hit the shore.

I was the hero of Lewisporte that night, though I did not
refrain from giving Gus his full due. I understand that since my
pioneer effort, others have successfully met the challenge; but I
took justifiable pride in being the first. I have made longer swims
since, and have swum in more dangerous waters. But to a 16-year-
old boy it was one of the peaks of his early life.

While I was teaching in Bonne Bay in the early 1930s, I had
proposed to my friends a climb of one of the lesser mountains as a
preliminary to undertaking one of the giants such as Gros Morne
or Table Land, but had detected a lack of enthusiasm. Their
reluctance was likely related to an avalanche that had swept down
one of the mountains some years before, taking a house off its
foundations and dumping it into the bay; four people had been in
the house, and only two of them, a woman and a baby, had survived.

But I was determined to go for a climb, and so on a fine afternoon when school was closed, I casually sauntered into the ravine,
which, though now dry, could become a raging torrent very
quickly. I took a few minutes to size up the geography of the area
and then decided the best route was the side of the main stream.

By using small trees, shrubs, and bushes, in less than two hours
I had completed my climb to the top of Coombs Hill and could
look out over the whole of Bonne Bay and the coastline stretching
from Rocky Harbour north to Cow Head and other places. It was
a feast for anyone's eyes.

When I wanted to return, I realized I did not have much time
until dark. I had told no one where I was going and if I got stuck
on my way down the peak it was not likely anyone would think of
looking for me on Coombs Hill. If I had to spend the night there,

with only the lightest clothing, it is doubtful that I could have survived the sharp cold of the mountain. I had no matches or other
means for starting a fire.

I reasoned that if I had climbed the peak in less than two
hours, I could go down much faster. The mistake I made then
was in deciding to return by means of the dry riverbed where the
sides were precipitous and where there was no vegetation to grab
onto. I had to take some grave risks, including the possibility of
starting an avalanche which would sweep me into oblivion in
seconds.

I managed to get down the peak without injury, and less than
one hour after I had begun my descent, just as it was turning
dark, I walked into Mr. Taylor's house to be greeted as a near-
hero. Actually, I had not been heroic but stupid. I should not
have tried to go up or down a dry riverbed in mountainous ter-
rain; I should not have climbed that massive hill without a companion; I should not have gone mountain-climbing, even for a
short distance, without warm clothes and simple survival equipment like matches and a flashlight; and, most of all, I should not
have left without seeking advice from local people regarding
safety measures and how to avoid unnecessary risk. I had done all
of these things and, as a result, almost paid with my life.

Extract from a letter to me written by Mr. Ralph E. Evans of
Musgrave Harbour in 1968:

> I may state that the Evans whose life you saved while he was swim-
> ming in Freshwater Bay near St. John's was my brother. He
> became a Salvation Army officer and is now Major Arthur E.
> Evans of Toronto, Ontario.* This incident is remembered by the
> family and they feel deeply indebted to you.

The incident referred to by Mr. Evans took place in July 1936
when the summer school at Memorial University was in full swing.
Among the social activities was an outing to Freshwater Bay, an
area between St. John's and Cape Spear. About 50 of the group,
including me, were ashore dressing after having gone swimming.
I was all dressed except for my shoes when I saw someone quite a
distance from shore who appeared to be in trouble.

I ran quickly to the water and dove in, but when I got to where

---

* Major Arthur Evans is now deceased.

I had last seen the person, I could find no trace, so I went under-water some ten or eleven feet. Then I saw something white, which turned out to be Evans's hand. I swam to the surface with the victim, who appeared to be conscious enough to understand my order for him not to touch me. (The danger in rescuing poorly-trained swimmers or nonswimmers is that they will get a death grip around your neck.) I turned him on his back in front of me, put his two hands on my shoulders, and allowed his head to come in over my shoulder and his body to straighten out between my legs in such a way that he did not impede my swimming ashore.

He had swallowed quite a bit of water, but vomited much of it up. He was indisposed for only a day or two and otherwise showed no ill effects.

chapter
18 *Political Vignettes*

PRIME MINISTER HAROLD WILSON

*I*t was just after the Six Days' War in 1967. Smallwood was in Europe and I was acting Premier. Without any warning, a call came through from Prime Minister Pearson's office saying that Prime Minister Wilson was leaving England the following day to fly to Washington so that he could confer with President Johnson on the Israeli war and other matters, and that he would be stopping at Gander for several hours. Could I arrange to go out to Gander to meet Wilson? Of course I said I would be glad to.

The next day Wilson arrived in his Comet jet. He was accompanied by Mrs. Wilson, and ministers and advisers of whom the most interesting to me was Sir Solly Zukerman, described by Beaverbrook as having the best brain in Britain.

I had seen Wilson in action on at least two occasions in the British house of commons and was very happy to meet him personally. We toured the Gander terminal (something in which he seemed to take more than usual interest). After tending to these chores we repaired to the distinguished visitors' apartment for refreshments and an hour or so of conversation. For my part, I was not slow in taking advantage of the opportunity to ply him with questions. One part of the conversation went approximately as follows:

Wilson: I suppose you live in St. John's, Dr. Rowe.
Rowe: Yes, I do. Have you ever visited it?
Wilson: No.
Rowe: You have a lot of headaches these days, what with the Middle East situation, the *Torey Canyon* wreck,* and so on. What would you regard as the most serious problem facing you?
Wilson: (jokingly) Where to find a new poet laureate. [John Masefield had died a few weeks earlier.]
Rowe: What is the difficulty there?
Wilson: There aren't any poets left.

Here he obviously did not mean to be taken seriously, for only a few days later he appointed Sir John Betjeman to the post.

   Another conversation of special interest to me followed:

Wilson: I suppose you or your people came out to Newfoundland from the West Country.
Rowe: Yes, most of the Rowes apparently came out from Devon and Dorset.
Wilson: I thought so. You resemble some of the Rowes still there.

Here I felt that he was stretching a point to make me feel good. But he appeared quite serious, and I was quite pleased when he continued on the topic:

Wilson: In fact, one of my best friends is a Rowe in Devon. He is a motorcar dealer and I have bought some of my cars from him.
Rowe: That's most interesting to me. But I don't suppose that, as Prime Minister, you get much time to visit Devon?
Wilson: Oh, yes. You see, our country home is on the Scilly Islands, and we go down to Devon by train to take a boat out to the Islands.

I could have kicked myself for my stupidity, for I had known about his home in the Isles of Scilly for many years. But there was more to come.

---

* The oil tanker had run ashore and had broken up only a week or two before, with oil washing up on the English Channel coastline.

Wilson: Were you born in St. John's, Dr. Rowe?

Rowe: No, Prime Minister. In fact I was born in a small town — a village then. Lewisporte is the name.

Wilson: Is that so? I know it well.

Rowe: Pardon me, Prime Minister, we're mixed up here. I was speaking of a Newfoundland village 30 miles north of here.

Wilson: Yes, I know it well.

Rowe: But I understood you to say earlier you had never been to Newfoundland.

Wilson: No, I said I had never been to St. John's. But during the war, I served in this area for a while and got to know Botwood, Lewisporte, Gander, and other places in the area quite well. In fact, I was glad we could come here to Gander to refuel, since it gave me a chance to look around the new airport and compare it with the Gander I knew in the early days.

And so ended a most fascinating conversation with one of the political leaders of our time. But the question arises: What was Wilson doing in central Newfoundland during World War II? I had tried to draw him out on this but he had seemed somewhat reticent. Perhaps I should not have wondered. Before World War II the British government had established a sea base at Botwood for transatlantic air travel using the flying boats. Also, before 1939, that government had started the construction in Gander of what by 1939 had become one of the world's great airports. But Gander was 30 miles inland, with rail but no highway connection, so as Gander became more and more important — with hundreds and in time thousands of planes needing to fuel there — Lewisporte became the great fuel reservoir. Without the tremendous contribution made to the war effort by these three strategic towns, the United States of America and Canada would never have been able to funnel their vast war effort to Britain, and later to western Europe. Perhaps Wilson's own war record hinged around these vital considerations. One thing is certain, in the life-and-death struggle of World War II, Wilson had not been simply a spectator; he, too, had served.

PRIME MINISTER LESTER B. PEARSON

Of the eight Canadian prime ministers whom I met during my lifetime, the one I learned to like most was Lester Pearson. This does not mean, of course, that I thought he was the best prime minister or the best political administrator—though I want to interrupt myself here to point out that any prime minister who could inherit a broken-down party and hold it together for four years or so, all the while making life miserable for the governing party, must have had something on the ball.

Pearson's period as prime minister coincided with mine as president of the Canadian Good Roads Association, a vast organization comprising every person and body connected in any way with building and maintaining the roads. The year 1964 was our Golden Jubilee year, to be celebrated at the Queen Elizabeth Hotel in Montreal. The choice of principal speaker was up to the president. In view of the tough period that Pearson had gone through, and feeling certain he would not take political advantage of the invitation, I thought we should invite him for this august occasion, and my feelings were shared by the rest of the executive. Pearson gave one of the most eloquent speeches of his career and received encomiums from guests of every political persuasion.

Before and after the formal proceedings, and during the dinner and presentations, Pearson and I had a number of intimate conversations about politics. Whether it was the nature of the function itself or a reaction to a decision he had recently made, Pearson was in unusually good spirits and chatted quite freely about matters that normally would have been left out of the conversation. Here I shall relate two examples that, in the light of subsequent developments and revelations, I am sure he would not object to my using.

We were talking somewhat flippantly about politicians and their good and bad points when suddenly he seemed to draw himself together and become more serious: "You know, Fred," he said, "there are very few persons that I have ever really disliked. In fact I can think of only one." He stopped and seemed to be looking into the distance. For a moment I hesitated, and then I said, "We're both thinking of the same man, aren't we?" "I think so," he answered, and that was the end of that part of our discussion.

Pearson also let me in on his future political plans. While chatting about retirement and related topics, Pearson quite casually said, "Well, I'm getting out next year." I thought that in the hubbub I had not heard correctly and said so, but he repeated his words. For a moment I was stunned. He was just finishing one of the most fruitful periods in Canadian political history, and here he was now about to enter the pantheon of elder statesmen! I pressed on him the fact that, without doubt, not only his Liberal following but thousands of independent voters would be grieved to know he was leaving, and other arguments, but it did not seem to have much effect. I then asked whether he was stepping down because of his health but, ironically, he dismissed that out of hand. "No," he said, "it's not my health. I'll be 70 next year, and I'd hate to stay on after that because then I might not want to get out."

QUEEN ELIZABETH II

During my lifetime I have met our present Queen probably a half-dozen times, the meetings consisting of a bow and handshake for the most part. There was one exception, however, and it occurred on one of the occasions when the Queen was visiting Ottawa for the purpose of opening Parliament. It was getting late in the afternoon and the Speaker of the House of Commons was taking the Queen from the Library through the Hall of Remembrance to the exit. My wife and I were walking through the Hall on our way to my office, and it was quite clear that if we waited we would almost for a certainty meet the Queen again. Whether it was thought we were trying to engineer a meeting I do not know, but at any rate the Speaker guided Her Majesty to our side, introduced my wife and me to her, and then stepped back a discreet space or two.

I had always known that one does not ask questions of the Queen; she is the one who initiates discussion. Nevertheless, I committed this blooper—and got away with it. To explain both these departures from protocol, some background is necessary.

On then-Princess Elizabeth's first visit to Newfoundland in 1952, the weather for her return trip was very stormy, with rain, wind, and rough seas. But she was to board one of the *Empress* ocean liners that the authorities were not willing to have come into St. John's Harbour, so there was no alternative to her taking an old and somewhat decrepit ferry, the *Manico*, that was used for crossing the "tickle" between Bell Island and Portugal Cove. The hundreds of spectators who braved the elements to have a last look at this courageous and lovely lady were appalled as they saw the ferry boat do everything except turn over, something that everyone expected momentarily. But the boat survived, and after some difficulty the Princess was able to get on board the huge liner.

Now here we were, 30 years later, making conversation with the Queen as she asked me a few things about Newfoundland. And then I heard myself blurting, "Does Your Majesty remember your first trip to Newfoundland?"

I realized my blunder immediately, but instead of giving me the cold shoulder as I expected, she suddenly became quite voluble on the whole affair. "You ask me do I remember? How could I ever forget? That terrible storm and that little boat! I made up my mind then that when I came back to Newfoundland again it would be by plane."

DONALD GORDON

One of the men connected with Labrador whom I found most interesting was Donald Gordon, former president of Canadian Pacific Railway, and then for a period president of the Churchill Falls project in central Labrador. (Gordon had several interests in Newfoundland, including the fact that his first wife was from a St. John's family.)

When the cornerstone for the Churchill development was laid, all those who had had connections with the great project were flown into Churchill for the ceremonies, but had to be accommodated at Goose Bay Airport for the night. In view of the very large number of guests, the base had no choice but to put two beds to a room. My recollection is that Smallwood and Winston Churchill (the grandson) were in one room and Gordon and I were in the adjoining room.

Gordon was a huge man, about six foot six with a big build. He loved Scotch and apparently could drink tremendous quantities of it without ill effects. But the one requirement for his successful drinking bout was that someone be present who could listen to his rambling conversation. Thus, instead of getting to sleep at midnight or thereabouts, I found myself conscripted as an unwilling audience — not because he was uninteresting but simply because I was dead tired after such a long day.

During his unending talk there was one brief lull when he turned to me suddenly to ask, "Rowe, do you snore?" I replied that while, like most people, I may have snored "the odd time," as far as I had been able to find out from my wife I was not a consistent or annoying snorer. "I'm glad to hear that," he said, "I don't snore myself and I hate like hell to be in a room where someone else snores." Having straightened out that matter he promptly fell asleep.

Then, to quote one of Gordon's own favourite expressions, "All hell broke loose." I have heard heavy snores on the many times when I have been an involuntary audience, but nothing remotely resembling Gordon's. His body — all 300 pounds of it — shook; his large bed shook; the building we were in shook. In fact, judging from the queries the next morning nearly everyone in the building must have been disturbed.

I did manage to get some sleep, and the two of us woke up around the same time. His first words, before I could speak, were: "Rowe, you son of a bitch. I thought you said you didn't snore. You kept me awake the whole night."

CHARLOTTE WHITTON

Just about everyone in Canada knew Charlotte Whitton. She had been a leading welfare figure for many years, a record that led her to become president of the Canadian Welfare Council. After retiring from the welfare field, she successfully competed in the Ottawa mayoralty elections, becoming Ottawa's first woman mayor. There, as in other areas, she was noted for her acerbic wit, which contributed to her sharp debating style. I don't think that she ever permitted her political views to interfere seriously with her duties to Ottawa and to her country; but most people who had dealings with her learned to fear her tongue, which she brought into battle whenever there was an opportunity.

My first contact with Charlotte occurred shortly after Confederation, when I was Newfoundland's first Deputy Minister of Welfare. She made no secret of her Progressive Conservative political inclinations and her sharp dislike of those of us who were Liberals. A chance to put me in my proper place came on an occasion when Lord Beaverbrook, C. D. Howe, and I were travelling and happened to be waiting at Fredericton Airport for our luggage. We caught sight of Charlotte, and at Howe's request she joined our little group and chatted vivaciously for the few minutes we were waiting. When the luggage came, she and I moved along through the airport to where a limousine was waiting to take us (so I assumed) to the Lord Beaverbrook Hotel in Fredericton. By now she and I were deeply involved in an argument. We had not gone far (fortunately) when she made a reference to Saint John, New Brunswick which aroused my curiosity. The conversation then went along these lines:

Rowe: Mayor Whitten, you just said Saint John, but I assume you mean Fredericton.

Whitton: No, I don't mean Fredericton, I mean Saint John.

Rowe: Aren't you mistaken? The Canadian Education Association is meeting here in Fredericton.

Whitton: Look, Rowe, how did you manage to get that idea in your head? I'm speaking to the Union of Municipalities in Saint John, and we're on the way there now.

Rowe: My God, Charlotte. I'm supposed to be in Fredericton for the annual meeting of the Canadian Education Association.

Whitton: Driver, turn around, will you, and take this man back to the Lord Beaverbrook — he's like all those bloody Liberals, he doesn't know where in the hell he's going.

JUDY LAMARSH

The period from 1950 to 1970 was one of tremendous development for western Labrador. The great railway, the most modern in the world, was completed by 1954, and two modern, sophisticated towns were built side by side to meet the needs of the two separate mines. Labrador City and Wabush were demanding attention of every sort, rightly feeling that since the companies and the residents had provided just about everything under the sun for visitors — hotel, swimming pool, ski slope, shopping centre, airport — everything except road connection with the outside world — it was not asking too much to expect a few ministers from Ottawa and St. John's to be with them for a celebration of their progress.

Since I had been the member for Labrador for several years and was soon to become Minister of Labrador Affairs in addition to my regular portfolio (which was then Education, I believe), I received an invitation. I was acting Premier at the time and I encouraged several of any colleagues to come along over the weekend and participate in a number of the planned functions, which included skiing and skating. The federal government, Liberal at that time, received special invitations as well, and as a result three or four of them also showed up. That delegation was headed by the Minister of Health and Welfare, Judy LaMarsh.

It was winter and there was ice everywhere. As Judy was getting off the plane, she slipped and was left with a cut below her knee.

However, she was resolved to carry out her program, which included a visit to St. John's on the following night, when a huge function was planned and I, as acting Premier, was scheduled to speak.

By Saturday, the day of the function in St. John's, Judy's knee was not very good, and the doctors felt that she should rest in Wabush, so in late afternoon we set off for St. John's without her. I had no time to go home but went straight to the function, which, I believe, was being held in the Holiday Inn. As soon as I was called to speak, I plunged right into the heart of the matter with: "I have just been spending the weekend with Judy LaMarsh —" Well, that did it: the ovation must have lasted five minutes. Finally it let up a bit, and so I went on: "Judy asked me to tell you that her knee was not in very good shape—" Now there was a hysterical reaction that must have lasted ten minutes, and I gave up trying to describe Judy's tribulations.

She was a trouper and all Canada mourned when she died prematurely a few years ago.

HENRY FROST

The federal-provincial conferences in Ottawa were, for the most part, fairly easy events for the average minister-delegate. As a rule, the provincial delegation consisted of the Premier, several of his Cabinet, particularly the Ministers of Finance and the Attorney General, and normally two or three senior officials. A typical session ended between 5 and 6 p.m., and this was followed by a formal reception and dinner at Rideau Hall, the residence of the Governor General. During these functions, there was ample opportunity for ministers to get to know one another and also to obtain nodding acquaintances with the premiers.

Of all the premiers I saw at these conferences I think the one I enjoyed most was Henry Frost. He was a large man, affable and sympathetic, who wore a deadpan expression most of the time. Early in our relationship, I felt quite at ease with him, as did, I believe, all the Newfoundland delegation. At Rideau Hall and at other functions he often sought me out to wish me well. At first, I thought this attention might be due to the fact that so many Newfoundlanders lived in Toronto and its suburbs. But as time went on, I felt that Frost was above that.

In early 1959 Prime Minister Diefenbaker had gone to the House of Commons and announced that Canada was going to unilaterally throw Term 29 of the Terms of Union down the drain. All Canada, not just Newfoundland, was appalled by this decision. Later that year, a federal-provincial conference held in Canada in camera gave the premiers a chance to express their opinion about Term 29. No province was against it, and most of them, a majority of whom were Conservative, supported it. Frost, who recognized at all times that his province, Ontario, wealthy and powerful, had a continuing responsibility to the weaker ones such as Newfoundland, led the way. He turned to Diefenbaker, a fellow Conservative, and said, almost scathingly, "Prime Minister, why don't you give Newfoundland what she is asking for so that we can go on to other business." That, and the general approval from all the premiers, took the spirit out of Diefenbaker: obviously, not only were the Liberal and NDP parties behind Newfoundland, but vast numbers of Tories felt the same way. For Diefenbaker, it was the beginning of a long-drawn-out end. But I was never prouder to be a Canadian than when Frost, respected by all, demanded justice for Newfoundland.

During the latter years of Frost's tenure as Premier of Ontario, he found out that I had been the member for all Labrador for four or five years. For some reason, this seemed to arouse still more interest on his part. I remember sitting down in the reception area while he plied me with questions, particularly about northern Labrador. I found out that he had never been to Labrador himself, and asked him why. "No reason," he said. "I always intended to, but something always interfered." But then why the intense interest in Cape Chidley, Chimo, Mugford, etc.? "Well," he said, "when I was a teenage boy I came across some books by a Scottish writer—" and here I interrupted, "—by R. M. Ballantyne, a famous writer in the late 1800s and a friend of R. L. Stevenson. I ran into them in a lighthouse in northeastern Newfoundland and read them all when I was about 13." Frost shook my hand and said, "I did the same and you are the only person I've met who has read them all. You know now why I am so interested in Labrador."

chapter
19 *Newfoundland Mythology*

B efore dealing with some specific myths about Newfoundland, it is worth spending a little time trying to guess the
causes of this aberration in the human race of inventing fables.

Several factors come to mind. First, there is the desire to understand, to find a story which is somewhat acceptable rationally and
without which everything is blank. This probably does more than
anything else to create myths, since man does not want to be left
in the dark about certain matters. Another strong reason, to my
mind, is the failure of human beings to understand events at the
time of their occurrence; the result is guesswork and, as time goes
on, even outright invention. One has only to think of the voyages
of Saint Brendan, the accounts of which had to wait for perhaps
1000 years before becoming a permanent record. Though nobody
believes the accounts are infallible, everyone believes that there
are large elements of truth in them. There is so much that we now
understand in the geographic sequences—birds, sheep, floating

marble columns, monsters of the deep, savage demons hurling red-hot lumps of fire into the ocean in attempts to destroy Saint Brendan — that Brendan or *someone* had to see those phenomena; no one could invent these accounts with such remarkable coincidences. How could Brendan know that Hekla and other volcanoes were waiting with their balls of fire?

Another reason for the growth and spread of mythology lies in the desire of many people to heap unflattering propaganda and outright lies on the heads of political or religious enemies. This occurred in Newfoundland for several centuries while the English and Irish fought for superiority.

Newfoundland is particularly rich (if that is the word) in mythology of all sorts. Any country with so many accidents in its background is bound to carry a heavy mixture of fact and fiction, and the tendency is especially evident with a reliance on word-of-mouth transmission.

An article in *Maclean's* magazine once told how Newfoundland fishermen encouraged shipwreck so that they would be able to salvage the unfortunate vessel or what was left of it. The best answer is to give a factual account of the Labrador fishery.

Early every summer, hundreds of schooners, driven by wind power, went to Labrador to fish, and returned in the fall. It was one of the most hazardous occupations on earth; every year, schooners were wrecked and lives were lost. In 1906, for example, my father had his schooner wrecked in a great hurricane that destroyed 26 vessels at Twillingate, leaving only one to ride out the hurricane. Yet not one life was lost. Why? Largely because the men on shore, at grave risk to themselves, helped to rescue the crews. Nor was anything taken from any of the ships until such time as the wreck authorities under the magistrate and other wreck officials (the Commissioners for Wrecks) declared the schooners impossible to save — something that happened only when a ship could not in fact be saved.

My father was shipwrecked another time when, in northern Labrador, a hurricane left him with no choice but to put his ship ashore in order to save the lives of the crew. Again, at grave risk to the residents, my father and his crew were rescued. This was a common feature of the Labrador fishery.

Some Newfoundland mythology is harmless and need not worry us. An example is the account of the loss in 1919 of the coastal steamer S.S. *Ethie* on the west coast, just north of Bonne

Bay. About all it did, apparently, was enable some person on the coast who owned a mongrel dog to claim that his animal had saved the people concerned.*

The facts are these. The steamer, whose chief officers were Captain English, Mate Gullage, and Walter Young—probably the leading authorities on west-coast matters in all Newfoundland at the time—got caught in a hurricane. It soon became clear that she could not withstand the wind and the logical thing was to select the best place to go ashore. When this was done, there was some difficulty about getting a line ashore so that a "bosun's chair" could be constructed. Eventually, however, the line came near enough for men on shore to retrieve the rope in their dories. As soon as Gullage had the necessary rope he proceeded with the chair, and once it was secured person after person was brought ashore until all 90 passengers and crew were safe.

The efforts of Gullage in particular were recognized by seamen everywhere. But inevitably the usual fiction was added: that a Newfoundland dog had swum out to the ship, seized the rope in his mouth, and come ashore with it; and this story, with its accretions, became a piece of Newfoundland folklore. Unfortunately, though it is colourful, it is not true. There was no Newfoundland dog anywhere on the west coast at that time. All the officers and passengers confirmed that it was the crew and the men on shore who effected the rescue.

In spite of all kinds of evidence to the contrary, tourist and other literature never fail to imply that the average Newfoundlander spends a great deal of time trying to locate, among other favourite foods, seals' flippers. Were Newfoundlanders used to eating seals' flippers? Yes. Do they still eat it? Yes. How often? Once in a blue moon.

For example, Lewisporte is on the northeast coast, and that means that Arctic ice in the spring is at most only a few miles out in deep water. Yet I would be surprised if very many residents ever go to the trouble of going out in boats, big or small, to try to shoot a young seal for the sake of the flippers, even though they do make excellent meat. I would be equally surprised if it were found that the average resident of Lewisporte has more than one meal of flippers a year.

---

* The story goes that he took the dog with him to the United States and there exhibited this noble animal to the American people, charging handsome fees along the line.

Another case where gross overstatement (perhaps understatement should be the word) prevails is with respect to the Newfoundland passenger railway. Everyone in the rest of Canada and in the United States "knows" what the "Newfie Bullet" was like: narrow gauge, unearthly twists and turns, cramped sleeping quarters, trains arriving routinely late, inability to handle snow, trains stuck for days and weeks, trains lashed to the rails, and so on. But here again, we have a core of fact surrounded by gross exaggeration.

First of all, let it be said that the Railway did suffer from being a narrow-gauge type, as did and does every narrow-gauge railway on earth. In Newfoundland's case, the system was built in 1881 and at no time was the country or province in a position to rebuild it. Also, the topography of Newfoundland was such that, without a rebuilt wide-gauge line, no other basic improvement was possible. But nevertheless, the Newfoundland Railway operated reasonably well down through the years. Having travelled on narrow-gauge lines in other parts of the world, I am able to state categorically that ours did not deserve to become an object of derision. The stories of trains being stuck in snowdrifts for weeks (and, in one story, months) as a matter of routine, were simply not true. For 40 years most of my travelling was by train, and it included having to cross the Gaff Topsail, the highest part of the line, many times; in all that time, only once were we stuck in a snowdrift for 24 hours. Over the years there were some instances of trains being stuck for several days or even weeks, but in general the record was not bad. It is probably a fact that Newfoundland's narrow-gauge was not stuck in snow any more often than western Canada's wide-gauge.

Another factor usually left out of the picture is that the Newfoundland Railway was one of the safest lines to be found anywhere, in spite of the lurid accounts of accidents carried from Newfoundland to the rest of Canada. My recollection is that between 1922 and recent years only one or two crew members have lost their lives.

The food on the Newfoundland Express was first-class, the linen immaculate, and the crew service in the dining car beyond reproach. The decision of the Canadian National to reduce and eventually eliminate the passenger service was not caused by defects, real or imagined. It was caused by the ever-recurring annual deficits. Had the service been profitable it would still be in use, fantastic tales and all, but it was called on to accept the same fate that other lines, both wide- and narrow-gauge, have had to assume.

At a more ridiculous level of mythology is the number of natives who by virtue of date or order of birth are alleged to be able to perform magical healing of minor afflictions. An anecdote from my own early life—an experience for which I am unable to offer a definite explanation—illustrates how such tales gain their credibility.

When I was ten or eleven years old, my hands became covered with warts—23 in all from the tips of my fingers to my wrists. Some of them were ugly and embarrassing, and several bled from time to time. Once when I was bleeding one of my classmates told me—in a quite matter-of-fact tone of voice—"Fred, why don't you go down to Aunt Annie's? She will cure your warts." I was as skeptical then as I am now, and resisted the advice for some time, though it was echoed strenuously by other school friends. But eventually, when even my mother felt there was no harm in trying, without telling anyone I went down to Aunt Annie's one Saturday morning.

"Aunt Annie, can you put my warts away?" I asked when she answered the door. "Yes, my son, come in." She led me to what appeared to be an almost unfurnished room, put a chair in the middle of the room, and then blindfolded me very efficiently. Next I heard her fumbling in a distant part of the room, after which she came to me and asked me to touch all my warts. She then touched each with some kind of substance that felt like salt beef. As she touched each wart she mumbled something— whether or not it was the same words in each case I do not know. She then removed the blindfold and said good-bye. There was no charge.

I went home and seemed to forget my warts—after several years of their being a nuisance. About three weeks later I happened to look at my hands and noticed that there was not a vestige of a wart anywhere.

What had happened? I don't know. I don't think there was anything psychological involved, since at no time did I have any belief in the process. But if I had been cured physically, then in what way? After much thought, my conviction is that in the cupboard—I did notice a cupboard in the area where she got the substance—she had a special soap or chemical of some kind that she applied to the warts. Whatever it was, I am sure Fred Rowe had no part in it apart from giving in to the badgering by his classmates, several of whom, incidentally, were Aunt Annie's off-spring.

My experience with Uncle Tommy was somewhat different. I was about 13 at the time and was suffering from a toothache in one particular molar. Three or four days had gone by without any lessening of the pain. There was no dentist in Lewisporte, and so I had the depressing choice of either suffering or going to the expense and nuisance of travelling to Grand Falls, some 40 miles away. But Providence intervened. As I was going from our house to the shop I looked up the road and there, trudging along, was Uncle Tommy, who lived about three miles away. Like a flash from heaven, I suddenly realized how stupid I had been. What had made me forget that Uncle Tommy was the seventh son of the seventh? He could stop nosebleed, cure headaches and tooth-aches, and perform miracles big and small.

There was one handicap, but I couldn't see how that would hurt. Uncle Tommy was stone deaf and everything had to be done by pantomime. I immediately turned and walked towards him with my mouth at the ready. I mimed and he seemed to understand, but just to be sure I took hold of his hand and pushed his finger in on the offending molar. The finger felt deathly cold (he didn't have long to live anyway), and he prob-ably had not washed for 50 or more years, but worse still, he had put his finger on the wrong molar and no amount of twisting and turning on my part could convey that to him. He simply looked into the distance and kept mumbling.

Once finished, he did not even look at me but reshouldered his burden and trudged on. I could only watch him go with utter consternation, for now, before he even reached the church hill, the wrong tooth was throbbing even more severely than the other.

What could I do? I had tried iodine, aspirin, various liniments, salt—in short, everything that every person in Lewisporte, young or old, had ever tried—and nothing had worked. The following Sunday I took the train for Grand Falls where the dentist, figur-ing that these were early molars, extracted them both!

chapter
20 *Characteristics of Newfoundlanders*

*D*uring my 16 years of association with Ottawa, Upper Canadians have frequently mentioned to me their puzzlement over the oratorical ability of so many Newfoundlanders, a number out of all proportion to the province's population. This number does not seem to diminish to any degree over the years either in the House of Commons or in the Newfoundland Assembly. Nor, for that matter, are our fine speakers confined to the legislative bodies. In fact, frequently it was the very obvious ability of certain persons that first drew them to the attention of the voting public.

Nor does the loss of some outstanding speaker leave a vacuum in that field. Just a few years ago Don Jamieson's rich baritone filled the House both figuratively and literally. But his political demise, followed not too much later by his tragic death, did not, as so many had feared, deprive the House of a proper spokesman for Newfoundland. Even before Jamieson had taken up his post in

London as Canada's High Commissioner, George Baker and Brian Tobin, to name only two, were drawing repeated acclaim from the other side of the House.

My colleagues and friends both in Parliament and outside of it have often asked me to explain this phenomenon, but I am afraid this is not easily done. We know, of course, that this is not some temporary, artificial development or a consciously planned operation; rather, it seems to emerge almost spontaneously with the need. As early as the 1820s and 1830s, observers saw the young orator Patrick Morris, and the older William Carson, step in where necessary and lead the Newfoundland people in their fight for political autonomy. And the process has continued all through the past century into the electronic age.

But the eminence of Newfoundlanders has not been confined to the field of oratory; it has extended to writing, theatrics, music both instrumental and vocal, and debating. As I write these lines, Newfoundland writers, actors, and choral groups are attracting national attention. And it seems likely that, here too, a perceived shortage apparently leads to attempts to remedy the situation, which implies the existence of some sort of reservoir.

Here I enter — not too seriously — into the controversy. It is an established fact that Newfoundlanders of Irish descent number between 35 to 40 percent of the population. But that figure, large as it is, does not give the true picture. What about all the people bearing such names as Williams, Walters, Jones, Roberts, Thomas, Lewis, and Matthews, to give only a few? It seems evident that a large number of our ancestors who have thought themselves of English descent are not English, but rather Welsh, which is another way of saying they are possessed of great artistic talent. One cannot go to Hyde Park on a Sunday night and listen to a vast Welsh choir without being conscious of the legacy that has been handed down to us.

I do not know what percentage of the Newfoundland people are Welsh, but certainly it is no small number. And that is nothing to be surprised at. Wales and the West Country are contiguous. Thousands of Welsh people over the centuries engaged in the West Country fisheries off Newfoundland and in time some of them gave up the practice of returning home each fall; the Williamses, Robertses, and Joneses simply stayed on, mingling their blood with that of the English and the Irish. There is, therefore, when we count all the Irish and Welsh, a sizeable majority of people of Celtic blood — a race whose artistic ability

has been a recognized part of our Western civilization and culture
for hundreds of years.

Newfoundlanders are often reluctant to acknowledge relationship with other Newfoundlanders of the same name. Why this
should be I don't know. The average Newfoundlander has little to
be ashamed of and much to be proud of, coming as he does from
a background that exhibits bravery and sacrifice of the highest
order. More than anything else, I suspect, the reluctance to
acknowledge relationship stems from simple ignorance of the
family tree. This factor is certainly to be found in the Rowe
family.

Growing up in Lewisporte I was aware of several Rowes. For
example, the Rowes had been fisherman-planters who came out
to Newfoundland to fish and who in time became settled in Newfoundland. One of the Edward Rowes of Trinity who had become
a magistrate for Trinity Bay became a shipbuilder in Trinity, an
occupation he had passed on to his son James who established a
branch in Hearts Content, which in time became the more important of the two branches. James's son Edward continued the
family business and his son, my grandfather, also named Edward,
moved from Trinity to Seldom, probably in the 1820s or 1830s.
There he founded the Rowe "dynasty," who have been prominent
in fishing for around 300 years.

There are few, if any, Rowes in Trinity today, for the simple
reason that they have left Trinity to go to St. John's, Toronto, or
numerous other places in Newfoundland, Canada, or the world.
Only recently I was talking with a director of one of the chartered
banks of Canada who told me that the head of his bank in the Far
East was a young man named Rowe who had been born in Seldom, and asked me whether I was related to him. My reply was
quite dogmatic: "Of course I am. I can't be unrelated, since the
young man is a direct descendent of my grandfather Edward
Rowe of Seldom, the first Rowe to reside in that community."

In this connection the reader may recall an anecdote given
earlier. When I first attended Memorial University College in the
early 1930s, one of the pre-med students there was Duncan Rowe
of Hearts Content. When I was asked by a third party whether the
two of us were related, I answered with assurance, "Oh, no. Dunc
comes from Hearts Content, while I come from Lewisporte."
Dunc's reply to the question was the same. But, as I explained in
the chapter on the Rowe family, we were wrong.

One incident that I still remember after many years relates to a village stretched along a coastline where I was visiting for the first time. As usual, I started at one end of the village and stopped at every home to the last. The occupants of the first several homes told me their name was Browne. Other names intervened until I reached the last several homes. Here, too, the name was Browne, and I hastened to tell the second group that I had already met some of their kinsmen. But the reaction was quite negative. They were not related! I did not insist, but it was clear to me that there had to be a very definite connection. That a half-dozen families would leave England or Ireland at the same time and come out and settle in a not-very-prepossessing outport in Newfoundland, bearing physical likeness and the same family name, without being related, was astronomically against the odds.

A symptom of the ignorance about one's family tree is the common mythology frequently used to give an account of the settlement of Newfoundland. When two Newfoundland men, after chatting for a while, endeavour to identify their ancestry, it is likely that without any hesitation one will explain his background to the other somewhat along these lines: "Three brothers came out from England, one settled in St. John's, another in Twillingate, and a third in Bonne Bay." Usually the three places concerned are at a goodly distance away from one another. Moreover, the number is almost always three, not two or five. And it is always three brothers, not father and sons, or three cousins, or any of the other possible variations.

Not many years ago I ran into someone who did not know what my family background was. It turned out that he was a Rowe. Without revealing my own, I asked him what his Newfoundland background was. Without hesitation he gave me the mystical three. He judged the separation to have occurred as much as 100 years ago. Since the clerical, judicial, and religious records of the Rowe family in Newfoundland go back to the 1700s, clearly this particular member was not to be commended for his research.

A phenomenon that has never ceased to astonish and mystify students of Newfoundland culture is the role that small, isolated communities have played in creating and maintaining high standards of living in virtually every sense of the term. How is it possible that communities could continue to maintain good homes, good nutrition, good schooling even in a one- or two-room school, and public services such as libraries, on such modest resources?

The mystery is deepened by the fact that often alongside these communities are others that have never been able remotely to approach their neighbours in the quality of home life, or in education at any level. The reasons for the discrepancies are not easy to untangle, but a brief examination of two such progressive communities should be of some value and lead to some tentative conclusions.

The places I have selected are King's Cove in Bonavista Bay and Moretons Harbour in Notre Dame Bay. First some similarities and differences. Both were fishing communities; both are relatively small, probably with only 300 or 400 people when they were at their peak. Moretons Harbour is on an island while King's Cove is on the mainland of the Bonavista Peninsula. King's Cove had a train service for nearly 80 years while Moretons Harbour had to rely on the service provided by the coastal boats and by a number of small passenger boats. In its heyday, each was the centre for large commercial enterprises which outfitted fishermen for the inshore codfishery, the Labrador fishery, and the seal fishery.

Now for a brief overview of Moretons Harbour. As far as I have been able to ascertain, at no time did its school have more than two teachers, and for long periods there was only one. Much of Newfoundland's history provides statistical evidence that in the one-room schools a student's attempt to do any great amount of high school work resulted in frustration, and in most cases a waste of time. Yet this was not so in the Moretons Harbour school, or in a dozen or so other schools in the sole-charge category. Moretons Harbour consistently turned out qualified high school graduates who went on to take teacher training, and later more advanced work. This little place can boast of having produced 19 or more fine teachers and clergy who now pursue their calling all over Newfoundland and Canada. From this small community have come Dr. A. G. Hatcher, first president of Memorial University; Dr. Chester Small, a nationally recognized professor of chemistry at Acadia University; and Colonel C. D. Wiseman, world head of the Salvation Army. Colonel Wiseman is one of the best known of the group, but at the same time, there are to my knowledge five other distinguished clergy, three of them Methodist (United Church), one Salvation Army, and one Anglican.

And while teachers and clergy were establishing their remarkable record, nine young women became registered nurses; one young woman became a dietician; one young woman became a social worker; one young woman became a professional musician; this woman's brother became a distinguished federal trade commissioner; two professional engineers became head of their respective government departments; two young men became medical doctors; one young man became a bank manager; and, to cap it all off, one young man became a politician and a minister of the Crown.

Despite the risk of making serious omissions, here is a list of distinguished names that come to mind: Brett, French, Jennings, Knight, Locke, Penney, Small, Stuckles, Taylor, Cornick, Osmond, and Woolfrey. Most of these names are old and are to be found throughout Newfoundland.*

Let us now examine our other example, King's Cove. This settlement came to the attention of the famous Irish Protestant entrepreneur, James McBraire, who was established in St. John's and Carbonear but needed more room for carrying on in northeastern Newfoundland to be near the fish and the seals. To carry out his plan, he brought out recruits from the British Isles, especially Ireland. He regarded King's Cove as his pet enterprise and tried in every way to provide services that could compare with the services his other undertakings provided.

After McBraire's return to England and his subsequent death, the enterprise did lose some of its momentum, but contrary to the pattern of most recruitments of this kind, the early settlers tended to remain in the community. (One father-and-son doctor team remained in practice for 80 years.) If it did become necessary for some to move, links with the old home in the Cove remained real and vigorous. The result was that King's Cove preserved some of the drive that encouraged the residents to remain and to make contributions of one kind or another even up to recent times.

In the present century, one of Newfoundland's biggest commercial enterprises originated with Gerald S. Doyle of King's Cove, who dealt in medicinals and cosmetics. Other substantial undertakings whose originators hail from King's Cove are those of: the Devine family; the Lawtons, who founded the well-known medical group of doctors and nurses; the Browns, who became labour leaders and politicians; and Dr. Arthur Sullivan of Memorial University.

---

* Moretons Harbour has not enlarged appreciably in recent years; the population tended to spread out to other places — Moretons Harbour is only a few miles from Twillingate and Fogo — to compensate for the incremental growth at home.

Aiden Maloney deserves special mention. He was one of the most distinguished of King's Cove's many sons and daughters, becoming successively a fish plant manager, a cabinet minister and first president of the Canadian Salt Fish Corporation (a component of the federal government's national fisheries policy).

Such are the nature and the obvious achievements of two and, as I say, perhaps an additional dozen or more communities that at first might not be considered capable of anything so remarkable. What explains it? I have thought about this question many times and have come to the conclusion that there are a number of factors involved. Chief among them are:

- A superior type of first settlers
- Dedicated clergy
- Dedicated teachers
- Merchants whose goals are not confined to money
- Initiative in the exploitation of surrounding resources — i.e. in growing crops, raising cattle and poultry, etc.
- A policy of encouraging students in the conviction that they count in the scheme of things
- The inspiration provided by such medical missionaries as Rev. William Kirby

The surprising fertility of places like King's Cove and Moretons Harbour should not, however, lead us to slight the contributions — both acclaimed and unsung — of the hundreds of other little communities across Newfoundland. In all of these can be found fine men and women with the special characteristics that make our province distinctive in so many ways.

Index